D0421824

The Absent Moon

The Absent Moon

*A Memoir of a Short Childhood
and a Long Depression*

LUIZ SCHWARCZ

Translated by Eric M. B. Becker

PENGUIN PRESS
NEW YORK
2023

PENGUIN PRESS
An imprint of Penguin Random House LLC
penguinrandomhouse.com

Originally published in Portuguese as *O ar que me falta* by Companhia
das Letras, São Paulo.

LIBRARY OF CONGRESS CATALOGING-IN-PUBLICATION DATA

Names: Schwarcz, Luiz, author. | Becker, Eric M. B., translator.
Title: The absent moon: a memoir of a short childhood and a long
depression / Luiz Schwarcz; translated by Eric M. B. Becker.
Other titles: O ar que me falta. English
Description: New York: Penguin Press, 2023.
Identifiers: LCCN 2022026195 (print) |
LCCN 2022026196 (ebook) | ISBN 9780593490723 (hardcover) |
ISBN 9780593490730 (ebook)
Subjects: LCSH: Schwarcz, Luiz—Mental health. |
Schwarcz, Luiz—Family. |
Schwarcz, Luiz—Childhood and youth. | Manic-depressive
persons—Brazil—Biography. | Manic-depressive illness. |
Depressed persons—Brazil—Biography. | Depression, Mental. |
LCGFT: Autobiographies.
Classification: LCC RC339.52.S375 A3 2023 (print) |
LCC RC339.52.S375 (ebook) |
DDC 616.85/270092 [B]—dc23/eng/20220802
LC record available at https://lccn.loc.gov/2022026195
LC ebook record available at https://lccn.loc.gov/2022026196

Printed in the United States of America
1st Printing

Designed by Amanda Dewey

For Lajos,
my grandfather

All that makes you laugh can make you cry,
it's just a question of weight
and size.

  —BILLY BLANCO (as sung by Os Originais do Samba)

I am ever a seeker, and this search
will always
be my word.

       —CARLOS DRUMMOND DE ANDRADE

Contents

CONTENTS

The Absent Moon

AT THE SUMMIT

The lift let us off at the top of the mountain, a spectacular vista, a white universe, beams of sun casting light and shadow over each notch in the alpine range. Everyone who arrives at that spot for the first time pauses for a few moments to take in the view. It is quite something to breathe in the pristine air, surrounded by snow on all sides, beneath our feet, and atop the farthest mountains. In such a vast space, the sensation that one is within reach of the sky makes each breath more intense.

Readying for the descent had always been a simple matter of taking a gulp of air to fill the lungs and letting a feeling of wholeness with the mountain come over me. But at that moment, for no reason I could understand, I felt nothing.

In fact, I could hardly breathe. I bent over to tighten

my boots, to conceal from my instructor—or myself—the anxiety that had stopped my breath and frozen my face. I dragged the ritual out only so I could catch my breath, trying to eliminate the knot that caused my throat to seize at the very moment I was expecting the opposite.

The pure air at that altitude and the speed of the descent had always been good antidotes to the depression I carry with me. I do not ski very often, but when I do, surrendering to the mountain's demands all day has a therapeutic effect, synonymous with joy and unwinding. High above it all, my only responsibility is to make the most of nature. The mood is the same whether I'm among snow-covered peaks or among other mountains I visit in Brazil, where I surrender myself to the chilly waters of rivers and waterfalls, powerless to correct their course, powerless to edit the details of my surroundings, powerless to assume responsibility for anything beyond my immediate control. The mountains demand humility, demand subservience to something that was not created by human hands. In return, they offer rapture.

But now, instead of rapture, I felt a kind of anguish, particularly ironic given the happiness of the occasion: my wife and I were taking our granddaughters, Zizi and

Alice, skiing for the first time. After exploring the faster runs in the mornings, I would be spending the afternoons with the girls, enjoying my front-row seat to their snowy adventures, and the late afternoons in merry conversation, games, and planning for dinner. Time with my granddaughters has long been a certain focus for me, in a life in which I have largely retreated from close friendships and limited my social interactions to people within my professional field, friendships circumscribed by the world of books, living much of my life in the company of family, or in silence.

It came as a shock to arrive at the peak that morning with my lungs seizing up and my breath short, an inexplicable dry knot in my throat, the total opposite of what I had spent months imagining.

It was not the mountain alone that demanded my humility. My depression required much more.

Startled by the effort required to fill my lungs with air, I wasn't thinking, at the beginning of this episode, of the day when I felt the first symptoms of depression. Few of us who are carriers of this illness are able to recall the exact moment when we first noticed its signs, surfacing at the moment we identify something between the throat and the lungs, an obstacle that blocks the airway, that makes the act of breathing difficult. In general, depression erases distant recollections; its own memory is short, exacerbating recent suffering, dismissing nearly all traces of history. It was this that I felt there at the top of the slope, and I never wanted to feel it again.

If I make an effort to recall when my condition first appeared, I am able to piece together some sort of narrative. I think back to my shortness of breath at the peak and suddenly I see the sad green eyes of my father, who never set foot there.

Even before the image of my father's green irises, the memory of my depression takes the form of a sound. The pulse of my depression is the sound of my father's feet banging against the bedpost in the room next door as he struggled to fall asleep. My dominant mental image of him, his eyes, green irises contrasting with his damp and reddened sclera—which filled his lower eyelid with water, the tears pooling—came later. First there was the heavy sound that came through the walls, *bang*, *bang*,

bang, bang, bang . . . This thud—almost the opposite of those eyes—was insistent and without rhythm. I cannot remember exactly when I heard his agonizing drumming for the first time, but I know this was the moment when my depression first made its presence felt. It was the first time I felt terror run through me, as I suspected that I would be unable to live up to my duties as an only child. It was the occasion when I realized, even at that tender age, that I would be unable to secure my father's happiness, and yet I was entirely aware that doing so would always be the most important mission of my life. A mission in which I failed utterly.

TWO

WHAT REMAINED IN
BERGEN-BELSEN

Thirteen and a half years after my father's death, any attempt to pinpoint the causes of his insomnia might well remain a gamble. Until I reached the age of seventeen, there was little I knew about my father's past, with one exception, which was the greatest of all secrets. André Schwarcz, the boy András—or Bandi, the nickname given to all Andrés or Andráses in Hungary—survived the war after fleeing the train that was taking him to the concentration camp at Bergen-Belsen. His father, Lajos, Luiz like me, was with him in the same car; he remained on the train and never returned from the camp. At the time, András was nineteen. Lajos was last seen alive when the Allies liberated Bergen-Belsen, but was too weak to walk or feed himself. My father learned this only in the

1960s, having spent more than two decades turning over in his mind how his father might have met his death. At the end of the barrel of a gun? On one of the "death marches" Jews were forced to complete between one train and another on their way to the camps? In the gas chamber? Of typhus?

Some of these circumstances would be related to me many years later. For our purposes here, we need only say that when I was still a child, my mother tried to explain my father's sadness—his difficulties sleeping, the sound of his feet hitting the bedpost at night. I learned the meaning of the word *guilt* from a young age, as something foundational to my existence, something more difficult to understand than my father's eyes or his legs. His guilt for having survived when my grandfather did not, for not saving him or dying at his side, gave him no quarter, much less the sweet dreams that he and my mother wished for me each night as they tucked me in. My father likely could neither sleep nor dream because the past roared back as pure insomnia. When my parents bade me to sleep with angels, could it be they were referring to some angel who would protect my slumber from all manner of nightmares, from my father's thumping feet,

or the angel who would arrive to save my paternal grandfather and finally permit my father and the entire family
to rest?

The order or the shove that Lajos gives András, and
which András consents to at a moment when the train
becomes stuck, will, with the years, translate into loud
thumping against the bedpost, into stifled tears during
Yom Kippur rituals, into difficulties expressing himself,
into fits of rage and grief. Spending an entire life beneath
the yoke of an all-powerful image, that of being pushed
to safety by his father, came at a great cost for André.
The night he told me the better part of his story, he
repeated, soul stirred, the words his father had told him:
"Run, son, run." Who can imagine what it means to show
obedience at the very hour when you feel in your heart
that being the good son means doing precisely the opposite, defying your father's order to escape and save your
own life?

András was the youngest and the only male child in
the family, and he felt all sorts of guilt in relation to Lajos.
He spent his life repeating that he had never been a good
son, that he had been a terrible student who caused trouble
at school; that his father was strict, and as a son he had,

during his nineteen years under the same roof, brought considerable disappointment to the rug salesman from Budapest.

I know almost nothing about my grandfather. I know his profession, and that he was poor, religious, reasonably cultured, full of courage, and much too serious. In the only photo I ever saw of him, he cuts a terrifying figure, so piercing is his gaze. His relationship with his son was not good, but Lajos, though strict, was calm, and spoke little and at a low volume. As I recall the fear his portrait inspired in me as a child, I imagine that he wielded his favor with a quiet authority, a magnanimity heavy with silence, and with an impenetrable gaze, difficult to withstand.

One time Lajos caught his son at the barbershop on Shabbat, getting ready to go to a tea dance, as was common at the time. Lajos said nothing until he saw András at home, when he revealed that he knew all about his son's activities on this, the most sacred day of the week for Jews, activities that were completely unacceptable for a rigorous observer of Judaism like himself. András was sure he would be lashed or punished severely. But Lajos merely told his son that he should have expected to be caught visiting a barbershop so close to home and that, should he wish to profane Shabbat again, he ought to go see a barber in another neighborhood. He must have spoken in such a piercing tone that András never dared go for a shave on another Saturday as long as he lived. Almost none of the details that I know about my grandfather came directly from my father, who rarely uttered the man's name. All that escaped from André's mouth was the remorse of a rebel son.

THE SCHWARCZ FAMILY CAME from Miskolc, one of the larger cities in Hungary, with its own sizable Jewish community. Our name, of German origin, was written in that country in an unusual way, with a *c* before the *z*. The spelling harks back to a time, perhaps during the Austro-Hungarian Empire, when Hungarian Jews, with an eye to reinforcing ties with Jews across Europe, imitated their then-compatriots by choosing names different from the locals', which most certainly was not a choice my grandfather made. The Schwarczes moved to Budapest when my father was only two years old. Though he had few possessions, Lajos was deeply respected in the Jewish community.

Another trait that belonged to Lajos, and also András, was fearlessness. The former paid for this with his life, the latter with guilt and depression. Only during the writing of this book did I come to know that once upon a time, father and son expelled from the environs of the building where they lived a group sympathetic to the Arrow Cross movement, a Nazi militia in Hungary. In Budapest, on the eve of the city's occupation by Eichmann's troops or perhaps even as they were moving in, there were wild swings in policies concerning Jews. At first, Hungarian leaders attempted to resist Nazi anti-semitic laws—generating a false sense of security among the local Jewish community. Over time, they began to yield, until the entire country was occupied by Hitler's army. Meanwhile, the political situation was in flux, and the persecution and oppression of Jews waxed and waned. During a brief interval when the Hungarian Nazis lost some of their power, András and Lajos, believing that the new situation would hold, told off the militia-men. But the cease-fire proved short-lived, and when the

Arrow Cross again took power, both were immediately rounded up and sent to the concentration camp. Revenge against the two men's brave act was handed down swiftly. The women of the family were spared, to demonstrate that the purpose of the sentence was to punish father and son for confronting the Nazis.

Lajos had already been courting risk by hosting Jewish services in a makeshift synagogue in his home. Details surrounding the clandestine synagogue in my grand-father's house—the house with the yellow star—came rushing back to my father's mind thanks to a statement by another survivor published in a Hungarian Jewish newspaper in the 1960s, which came into my family's possession via a distant cousin who spoke atrocious Portuguese and owned a butcher shop in the Bela Vista district of São Paulo. The article saluted the courage of the rug merchant who defied the law and invited Jews to continue their religious services in his own residence, at 43 Paulay Ede Street, refitted as an underground synagogue. In the article, the survivor also mentioned that András and his two sisters would help to prepare the home for each service.

It was only some years later, near the end of the 1960s,

on a trip to Vienna, that André learned that Lajos had been seen alive when the Allies arrived in Bergen-Belsen, which lifted the weight of at least one of his long-standing fears.

I was with my parents on the occasion. I vaguely recall the encounter, at a pastry shop where a friend of my father's gave us the news, but often I think I must have dreamed my presence at such an important moment.

Lajos, an elderly religious man, had escaped the firing squad and the gas chamber. All the same, he hadn't had the strength to return to his family. They say that in his final days he was carted around on a stretcher, an exceptional thing inside a concentration camp, a sign of respect and admiration from peers for a wise man who would ultimately die of malnutrition and frailty.

I did meet my paternal grandmother, but I don't remember a thing about her. Yolanda remained in Hungary after the war, when my father went to Italy ahead of the rest of the family to try to arrange for their immigration to Israel. In the crapshoot that was visa procurement following the war, André ended up in Brazil, and my two aunts, Magda and Klari, both of them married, stayed with their mother. After some time, they decided to wait no longer for the documents my father had tried to obtain. In 1948, they fled to Australia. My father had already arrived in Brazil in 1947, before the country temporarily closed its doors to Jews. It was a time when everything was changing rapidly; official policies were subject to shifting winds that almost always blew against the Jews. Even with the defeat of Nazism, there was a long way to go until Jews were considered citizens of the world, with the freedom to emigrate, leaving behind them the lands that preserved the memory of their persecution.

According to my mother, when Yolanda's daughters departed, she herself was jailed and then put under house arrest. Punished for her children's illegal flight. This is one of the darkest moments in my father's family history. Freed six months later, my grandmother remained in Budapest for several years, coming to Brazil only in 1955 for my parents' wedding. The fact that each of her children followed his or her own path, leaving their mother behind in Hungary, was a common story among Jewish families during the postwar period, and led to a disagreement among siblings that would last for some time. My father took offense at Magda's and Klari's behavior, for having left without their mother. They would only speak again years later, thanks to my maternal grandfather. In retirement, André would go to Budapest for an annual encounter with his sisters. They would spend two weeks together at a spa resort, at the invitation of the youngest sibling, without any more hard feelings, having made a certain peace with their past troubles.

THERE IS A CURIOUS PHOTOGRAPH in my parents' wedding album in which my paternal grandmother is leading my father to the altar. Only my father is smiling. Yolanda stayed in Brazil for three years, living in a modest apartment in the city center. She refused to get together with my mother, who did not observe kashruth. Yolanda frequently complained that, in his house, my father did not observe strict religious rules governing food, and she invited him to dine alone with her on Shabbat. She would buy live carp to cook and kept them, for days, in the apartment's bathtub.

Yolanda underwent cataract surgery when she was in Brazil, and she had to stay in my parents' house during her recovery. She refused to eat any food cooked by my mother, who had bought new pans so as to follow the strict rituals of Jewish law and appease her mother-in-law. Mirta swore not to mix meat with milk or bring any sort of crustacean or pork into the kitchen. All the same, my father was forced to pick up food from restaurants in the Jewish neighborhood of Bom Retiro, where kashruth was rigorously observed.

Having failed to adapt to Brazil, Yolanda moved to Australia, where she went to live with her daughters. Ironically, Klari, my father's eldest sister, changed her name when she left Hungary and raised her son, Tom, my only cousin by blood, as a Protestant, without observing that or any other religion herself. So as not to appear Jewish, my aunt had undergone plastic surgery on her nose while still in Europe.

The Protestant ruse was very typical during the war and postwar periods, perhaps especially among certain Hungarian families. At the end of the 1960s, I came to know one such family that lived on the floor above ours in a building on Rua Alagoas. The couple upstairs and their only son maintained the deception for more than twenty years. Perhaps the boy, like my cousin, wasn't even aware he was Jewish. I'm not sure if they felt uneasy about our presence in the building, but after some time the neighbors openly reassumed their Jewish heritage.

With his religious grandmother's arrival in Australia, Tom, too, discovered he was Jewish. If Yolanda would not accept my mother's gentile cooking, what was there to say of her daughter who had never told her own son about his origins? The middle daughter, Magda, took it upon herself to provide strictly kosher food in her house so that Yolanda could eat with her family.

I HAVE NO WAY of knowing for certain whether my grandfather or my grandmother suffered from depression. If I had to guess, it's more likely it appeared on the female side. What can be said is that Mirta and André replicated the gap in culture in my grandparents' marriage, on a smaller scale and with the roles reversed. Yolanda wasn't at all well educated, while Lajos was considered a man of some culture. In my parents' case, Mirta was notably more attuned to cultural matters than my father.

During the nearly three years she lived in São Paulo, Yolanda scarcely left her apartment; she spoke only

Hungarian and in all likelihood saw very little of me. After spending some time with her daughters in Australia, she became sick and died of cancer. Klari always demonstrated depressive traits, a constant up until her death. Magda would spend a few more years in Australia and, after separating from her husband, immigrate to Israel, finally realizing the entire family's original plan. She was in no way depressive, and neither was my father, until he underwent his great trauma. Psychiatrists understand traumas to be one of the most common causes of depression, regardless of a person's genetic predisposition. This must have been André's case.

I would hear the wartime story of my father and my grandfather on only two occasions: when the article about my grandfather's clandestine synagogue was sent to my father, and many years later, in more complete form, one Shabbat. I was seventeen at the time. Shaken after viewing a documentary about the Warsaw Ghetto, my father finally decided to tell me everything about his past, a subject he would never again mention.

My father's image of himself as a bad son who obeyed his father when he should have rebelled deeply affected my sense of self. André was a generous and kind man. But my principal inheritance has always been guilt. If András was guilty of a double failure—frequently disrespecting Lajos's religious rigor only to later allow his father to save his life—I had to right the ship, save my own father from a life of sadness, provide a joy that the unyielding remembrance of the past rendered impossible.

I was a young boy when I first noticed the din that accompanied André's insomnia. I couldn't venture a guess as to my age. I'm also unable to pinpoint a date in my mind for the conversation in which my mother shared the origin of my father's problems: his nocturnal volatility; the wild mood swings, gentle one moment and unglued the next; his violent response the first times I misbehaved; and some of the psychiatric treatments he had undergone—which, as I remember, included electroshock therapy. André's pilgrimages to neurologists, psychologists, and psychiatrists would last for decades. He abandoned treatment a time or two, but never for long—without medication and close observation he could barely manage to close his eyes. Of a quiet, reserved temperament, he never shared details of his therapy, not even with my mother. For many years he took potent medicines for insomnia, such as midazolam and Rohypnol, more commonly administered today as preanesthetics.

I still feel the knot in my stomach or shortness of breath that I felt when learning of my father's debilitating condition. When I was young I did not know the meaning of the word *depression*, and I had yet to develop flagrantly depressive behaviors myself.

André always spoke softly, trailing off, but his voice was full of tenderness. Like every Hungarian, he would mix up the gender of words in Portuguese and place stress on the first syllable. He had a wide smile and a voice like butter. He sang gypsy tunes like a tenor in a Verdi opera. But when he lost control, his screams would echo throughout the house. The sense of dread brought on by the pounding of my father's leg and my fright at the verbal violence of his explosions typified the first moments when I felt the same shortness of breath or my throat locking up, as on the ski run. That was the moment when I learned what it means to live in fear.

THREE

THE SEPARATION

I can still remember the day when I was woken up and called to my mother's bedside. She was alone. I believe it was a Saturday. This was how I learned that my parents had separated. My shock at the separation and my lone figure at the maternal bed are my only memories of this conversation. From that day forward, I would see my father every other weekend, in his tiny apartment on the Alameda Barão de Limeira, not so far from Rua Bahia, where I was born and spent my early years. I would also spend afternoons testing out my skills as striker on whatever I could find for a soccer ball in the backyard of the Clube Húngaro, where my father would go play *remy*, a game akin to rummy with a Hungarian accent. I must have been about five years old. On days I was with André, in order not to completely miss his card game, he would leave me with other children for a few hours and tip the club attendant to keep an eye on me. Still, the memories I retain of these weekends are of my father's affection and dedication; he had not wanted to separate. On the contrary, André used me to try to coerce Mirta to go back on her decision and allow him to return to the apartment. Their divorce was quickly formalized. According to the settlement, my father had to leave me at the building's reception area and forgo any contact with his ex-wife.

I also remember two vacations with my mother during this period, which lasted a little more than a year. One longer trip, to the popular holiday town of Campos do Jordão, and the other brief, to Rio de Janeiro. I can still picture the meals at the Grande Hotel—especially the beef tea, a sort of meat juice that I was given to drink, likely because of my slight build—as well as the strolls along Copacabana Beach, where I gazed, eyes wide, at the goalposts anchored in the sand. Perhaps this is where my attraction to the position of goalkeeper came from, something that would take on great importance in my youth.

The hotel in Campos, which later was shuttered for decades, was not grand in name alone. It boasted pine forests, lakes with lily pads encircled by hydrangeas, a great number of rooms, and a pool that might not have been all that large but seemed so to my eyes. From my perspective, alone with my mother, everything was immense, as though we were two tiny specks in a universe that both fascinated and petrified me. Perhaps the leftover space ought to have been filled by my father.

The explanation I received for my parents' separation is lodged in my adolescent memory, not earlier. What I've learned about this time has been related to me over the years, and suggests a rocky marriage from the outset, a husband who was big-hearted but intellectually unremarkable and scarcely attuned to cultural affairs, with his group of Hungarian friends and leisure time centered on card games that lasted entire weekends. My mother, more cultivated and an admirer of literature and fine arts, didn't like cards, did not speak Hungarian, and had little in common with the group that had arrived in Brazil along with my father. She considered my father's friends and their scene too dissolute, drawing a connection between the behavior of the Hungarian community and the practices of modernist Vienna, where, she claimed, "*haus freund*," a sort of ménage à trois, was common, most typically between two men and a woman. For Mirta, the stream of extramarital affairs arising at parties and good-timing husbands who gave their wives no satisfaction were the rule among couples in André's crowd. But several wives also maintained their freedom in this area, something that was never in my mother's plans. There were considerable differences, in her view, between her and her husband's attitudes toward marriage. My father refused to give up his card games, while Mirta longed for a different kind of relationship; she wanted a companion. Her solitude became unbearable.

The divorce finalized, my maternal grandparents made efforts to ensure a reconciliation never came about. They went so far as to enlist neighbors in the two buildings where we lived during this period to monitor whether my parents were seeing each other.

My mother was also an only child. My grandfather had forbidden her from studying medicine, her dream. In his eyes, the university was no place for women, not to mention there was the possibility that his daughter might fall in love with a non-Jew and get involved in the student political movement. Mirta was forced to take a secretarial course and work with her parents while she awaited marriage one day, when she would look after her new home. And that's what she did when she married André, the handsome devil she set her sights on from the first time she saw him, at a dance at the Clube Húngaro. Some years later, as my grandfather's secretary, my mother would see my father again at the family print factory, called Cromocart, where he often came around as a sales representative for a paper manufacturer. André frequently visited Cromocart, and initially he had an excellent relationship with my grandfather. When his daughter showed interest in the handsome and good-natured paper salesman, Giuseppe would exit via a side door whenever he saw André coming in the front door.

When they married, Mirta was eighteen and André thirty. Jealous, and doubtful of the sincerity of my father's love, my grandfather did his best to prevent their hasty union; he took my mother for a month's vacation in Europe in an attempt to divert her attention and persuade her to give up her youthful passion. He was not successful.

Upon their return, Mirta demanded that her parents acquiesce to the match, and a date was soon set.

After they married, my father went to work with his father-in-law. It was a bad idea from the very beginning. The business that brought so much pride to my grandfather was the stage for daily squabbles between father- and son-in-law. There was no peace at the printing business where my own future was to lead. At times I dream that when I was born, my parents and grandparents fixed a welcome sign to the hospital room door, printed at Cromocart Artes Gráficas itself, with the message: WELCOME, DEAR HEIR, THE PRINTING BUSINESS ON AVENIDA RIO BRANCO AWAITS YOU. But in the meantime, the years passed slowly, until finally, with my parents' separation, my father left the business and my mother returned to work as a secretary, to help with the bills.

My parents would reconcile, but my grandparents never stopped interfering in their relationship. For a little more than a year, André continued to work at a clothier making girls' pleated skirts, a business he had started with Hungarian friends soon after the divorce. After this, paradoxically, my grandfather demanded that my father return to Cromocart, leaving his partnership in the modest clothier in the neighborhood of Bom Retiro, where he was very happy. The clothier was less lucrative than the job at Cromocart, but André's and Mirta's life had emerged out from under the long shadow cast by the tense relationship between father- and son-in-law. However, they relented to pressure to return, assured that my grandfather would soon retire. This was one of the few promises that Giuseppe came nowhere near fulfilling. As for my grandmother Mici, she pressed for her son-in-law's return because she wanted to go on trips with her husband, and they needed someone they could trust to mind the business. Giuseppe's tension with his son-in-law was a price she was willing to pay.

Though our family life outwardly appeared normal, my grandparents harbored a silent animosity toward my father that never faded. Every Saturday at lunch, or at dinners on Jewish holidays, we would go to Giuseppe and Mici's apartment on Rua Piauí, in front of Praça Buenos Aires, and later to their place on Rua Pernambuco. Most of the time, no fights broke out, but something was missing in our intimate family circle; love was not distributed equally. The only thing those four adults had in common was the heir—me.

My grandparents also competed with my parents over me. The firstborn son and grandson became the target of overzealous pampering, particularly on Mici's part. She and Giuseppe treated me as though they were more than grandparents. It was as if I had two fathers and two mothers, all of them full of love to give. Over time, this would only grow worse.

At a very young age I was becoming one of the family's stronger personalities, second only to my grandfather. To the outside world, Giuseppe was a generous man, but he showed little regard for his wife and daughter, much less his son-in-law. When I was not yet a teenager, I became the only person he listened to.

And even before that, I had become the confidant to both my parents, a situation that began during their separation and grew worse with time. I felt caught between my father's complaining, my mother's doting, and declarations by both of their love for their only child. With their actions, they revealed their fragility to me, undisguised. Twisted in one direction and then the other, I wasn't sure I could rely on those who ought to have been my first heroes and role models in life. I took on an enormous sense of responsibility, aggravated by the fact that, from the time they got back together, I continually heard them say that they had done so on my account.

One Sunday when they were still separated, I was climbing the stairs to the apartment without my father, and when my mother greeted me at the door, my anger at her over our sad situation boiled over and I landed a punch smack across her stomach. Shattered, Mirta drank whiskey alone that night for the first time in her life and decided to ask my father to come back. That day, I was no doubt made aware of my childhood powers. Of course, there was something between my parents that was crucial to their reconciliation, but it is also telling that, nearly sixty years later, I still feel the responsibility squarely on my shoulders.

I BECAME A VERY SERIOUS and duty-bound son. That image of me stuck with my grandfather, who was already predisposed to idealize his grandson. It's possible that, thanks to our family dynamics, even had I not developed these personality traits early on, Giuseppe would have placed undue trust in me.

In the face of these unrealistic expectations, I also began to demand too much of myself. While this combination might not have saddled me with childhood depression, it certainly sharpened my sense that I played a crucial role in my parents' marriage and in keeping André from falling further into a deep melancholy. In the final decades of his life, he would place even more responsibility on me to save his marriage, which, except for a brief period following their reconciliation, would always be brittle. From a young age, this was my dilemma: I felt crucial to a marriage that had every reason to go wrong, and crucial to the happiness of a man I was powerless to make happy. Still a child myself, I lacked the means to understand any of this.

The image of myself that sticks from that time was taken by a professional photographer: slicked-back hair, neat clothes set out by my mother, sitting with my feet dangling in the air—they don't even reach the bottom of the sofa—at my grandparents' house. In my lap is a small guitar I could not yet play. The pose includes an angelic smile and a heavens-turned, faraway look.

Later my mother would make me pose for a portrait in oil. I was around seven years old. I spent hours dressed in a marinière, blue and white, a form of torture I submitted to without complaint. What can be seen in the painting, which today hangs on the wall of my granddaughters' room, is an adult boy, a steely-eyed mariner in the body of a child, who, unlike the boy in the photo, directs no smile upward, nor toward the portraitist.

In those years, when I would ask for a brother or sister, I received tortured responses from my parents. Only later did I come to learn that three or more siblings of mine never made it to birth. In fact, one of them was born, received a name and a burial. Others my mother lost along the way, due to either medical errors or health problems. Three was the number I was told many years after the events had come to pass. Today my mother speaks of perhaps a dozen miscarriages.

Mirta's efforts to become pregnant would last nearly a decade, including several months in bed, in a battle to avoid losing child after child. In her final attempts, when she spent a long time on her back, almost never on her feet, I was told the cause was an ulcer in her stomach. She did in fact have such a condition, but the story was more complex than that. I spent hours at her side, reading *The Fountain of Youth*, a treasury of stories, tricks, and games for young boys. The encyclopedia taught one how to make a slingshot or to swim, at least in theory—there was no water involved. Later I would draw on this time spent at my mother's bedside in writing a children's book, called *In Search of the Fountain of Youth*. Looking back, I think that this hefty blue tome was written for boys who, like me, had no friends but read classic fables and dreamed in their loneliness of what it would be like to play with others.

Whether working or when trying to get pregnant during those long years while looking after the home, Mirta always felt responsible for passing on to me an appreciation for books and art. I don't have many memories of her playing with me. The overriding image I have of my mother during my childhood is of her being bedridden. When we weren't having a conversation, our time together was spent reading, or looking at the booklets she collected about artists.

A short time later, during middle school at the Colégio Rio Branco, I made my first friend, by the name of Roberto Amado. He was the nephew of Jorge Amado, the great writer from Bahia. In Mirta's library, Amado occupied pride of place. She read everything that the author of *Captains of the Sands* published. One day, still bedridden, making an effort to bring one more pregnancy to term, she asked me to take a pile of books to Roberto's house, where Jorge Amado was staying temporarily. The pile of leather-bound books that I carried to the apartment on Rua Itacolomi could have qualified me to work as a circus clown. There, in the winter garden, I found a kindly man dressed in leather sandals, white Bermuda shorts, and a floral-print shirt. His belly won out against a few buttons of his shirt, popping them open. He was very friendly with me, but it took some time before I got used to the idea that that man, frumpy and without airs, was truly the great writer Mirta was always talking about.

AT ANY RATE, the images of me in the photo and in the painting and in the memories at my mother's bedside coalesce into a portrait of the early years of an only child who, from a young age and against his will, took on responsibilities hardly befitting someone his age. In the photo, the upward gaze would come to symbolize an exaggerated sense of self-importance that would overcome that boy, a miniature family messiah. Or perhaps it was a small cry of help to the heavens, stamped on the face of a child who would soon learn that such a messiah does not and would not ever exist.

FOUR

THE FIRST SIGNS

Those who suffer from depression live only in the moment. The verdict is always in the absolute and in present tense. Are we depressed or not? Beyond therapy sessions, we run from our memories and interpretations. As I try to reconstitute the prehistory of my disease, I find myself thinking about my constant anguish as a child. It was a time permeated by fear and silence. However, these feelings came out of nowhere; they felt natural, as though there were no particular reason for them. Without anyone to compare myself to, I likely thought that fear was an essential part of life, that everyone felt as I did.

Life was quiet, solitude was the norm, and underneath it was an all-consuming fear.

Later, in my teenage years, I now believe, my depression first reared its head. I had a strong propensity to sleep until the afternoon, during melancholic stretches that varied in intensity. At the same time, I was prone to wolfing down great quantities of food. It was common for me to eat an entire pizza. Today, I know that this combination can indicate an atypical variety of depression, and is a potential indicator of bipolar disorder. But I didn't see myself as depressed until I was fourteen, when a family doctor told my parents he thought I ought to see a psychologist. At the time, I wasn't yet active in my Jewish youth group. But soon, thanks to this group, I grew into something of a leader, shepherding the younger children with great energy and a certain charisma. I also became the starting goalie at my school, Colégio Rio Branco. During this period, my depression disappeared entirely. Before this time, I'd had few friends. At home, I spent my afternoons industriously doing my schoolwork; listening to music, a new habit that had burst into my life; and sleeping for hours and hours.

When I was a little younger, I had passed the time kicking a ball against the wall and then retrieving it, playing button soccer by myself on the table, and watching the passing cars through the enormous living room window, sitting on my knees in the sunroom covered in shag carpet and vase after vase of ferns. As I watched the cars, I would try to guess which would turn the corner, and I celebrated each time I guessed right, as if I had some ability to predict the future. I would also spy on the boys on my street as they played stickball or soccer with a stocking ball, never summoning the courage or self-assurance to go out and join in the fun. So I would lob Sonho de Valsa bonbons and Diamante Negro chocolates, filched from the pantry, toward the tiny playing field located in the empty lot next to our building. After tossing a candy, I would hide behind the curtain and watch as the children turned toward the heavens, trying to understand how it was that chocolates were falling miraculously from the sky. Noting the diminishing bonbons, my parents grew suspicious, and I was forced to curtail this pastime.

During the separation, my mother and I had moved to a smaller apartment. We left the comfort of Rua Bahia, that apartment having been sold as part of my parents' divorce settlement. When they resumed life as a couple, we remained on Rua Itambé, but Mirta once again left her place at the printing business and got a job to supplement my father's, at her insistence. I would sit at my mother's side while she sewed clothes for outside clients and accompany her on store visits. I had trouble understanding when buyers unjustly refused her delivered merchandise. This was not so uncommon in the 1960s—a woman who worked alone was often treated scornfully by rude and sexist shopkeepers.

My mother and I would have long talks during this period, on the most varied subjects, but family life was absolutely one of the central topics. We also spoke about the heroic feats of my maternal grandfather, who was responsible for rescuing the family just before the Nazis invaded Croatia, and about my father's troubles. It would be awhile before he went back to work with my grandfather. André lingered a bit at the clothier in Bom Retiro. The environment there was more his style, though it was definitely not my mother's scene. Her work selling skirts padded the family finances. This was the happiest period in their life together. My father was spared daily interaction with my grandfather, and my mother was occupied with her own job, and was responsible for more than the housework.

Their attempts to get pregnant were temporarily suspended and would only resume later on, when André returned to Cromocart and having a large brood again became the central aim of my parents' life. To this end, Mirta would stop working. The dining room table was freed up for my games of table soccer, but the environment around my imaginary stadiums changed, literally overnight.

For André, even lacking other children, at least one thing was already guaranteed: I would carry forth the name of my grandfather, in an attempt to restore a life lost to tragedy. And so I received a liberal Jewish education from an early age, attended the religious education course at São Paulo's Congregação Israelita twice a week, and was bequeathed the only possession my father had brought with him to Brazil: the tallit worn by my grandfather on High Holy Days. The tallit was a thick wool shawl—white with black stripes, the white having grown yellow with time—much too warm for a tropical climate. To this day, I feel something stir inside when I don Lajos's garment on Yom Kippur, the Jewish Day of Atonement. Jewish boys use the tallit only after their bar mitzvah. When I turned thirteen, I felt a combination of emotion and discomfort as I put on the prayer shawl that had belonged to my grandfather, of whom I knew very little. The emotion weighed on me along with the heat.

For my father, Yom Kippur was a day to honor his own father. Though he did not know the exact date of Lajos's death, he decided it had coincided with this sacred day. He would spend the entire day at the synagogue, fasting, as the strictest Jews do. Throughout the ceremony, his eyes would well up. I don't know how they bore for so many hours the weight of his dammed tears, nor how they could redden so abruptly.

This coexistence with such despair was painful. I wanted to get out of there, from my spot in the second row of the temple, a few feet from where the rabbis would sit. I twitched incessantly, casting a longing gaze toward the mezzanine above, where most of the children sat, with much greater freedom to talk among themselves. My father, who demanded I stay at his side the entire time, would poke me with his elbow and direct my attention to the prayer book with his index finger. And so the weight of my grandfather's death fell on my shoulders, too.

Aware that I would sweat like a pig in the tallit, my father would allow me to take it off except for during the most important prayer, Kol Nidre, at sundown. This part of the liturgy never failed to bring a flood of emotions, burning up or no, both for the beauty of the music and the repeated personal appeals for forgiveness, so meaningful to André. In the Kol Nidre, Jewish people ask God for forgiveness for their sins and for converting to other religions to survive the Inquisition. The melody is sung with the temple elders on the altar. This prayer opens the Day of Atonement, which concludes at sundown the next day.

If my father's sadness on Yom Kippur was palpable, it seemed to reach its zenith with the Kol Nidre. The first few years, covered in sweat, I would exchange Lajos's wool tallit for a lighter shawl my aunt had brought from Israel as soon as the opening prayer came to an end. Today, I insist on using my grandfather's tallit for the duration of Yom Kippur.

MY ROLE AS CONFIDANT to my parents, the weight of my grandfather's shawl, the excruciating hours at my father's side in synagogue . . . What would have changed if I had spent less time gazing toward the upstairs mezzanine and simply gone and joined the others, or gone to play with other children outside? What would my story be like if

I had found the courage to go down and play soccer with the boys from the slums near our building and shown them that, despite my sheltered existence, I was a gifted goalkeeper?

In a short story entitled "The Seventh Floor," from my book *Discourse on Some Blades of Grass*, I tell of the afternoons spent at the sunroom window on Rua Alagoas, watching the other boys play soccer. In the story, the main character asks himself whether he could manage to play barefoot as they do, or if he could withstand the embarrassment of wearing his impeccable leather tennis shoes. "The Seventh Floor" ends with the narrator taking stock of the time that has passed and of his own growth. In real life, because my childhood was cut short, I'm not sure whether I had so nuanced a relationship with the passage of time.

The brown shag rug and the floor-to-ceiling windows that characterized the modernist style of my third address in the heavily Jewish neighborhood of Higienópolis are but some of the images that I retain of a childhood bubble, apparently very sheltered and yet actually vulnerable to everything going on around me and which with time reverberated in the silence of my mind.

At moments when my depression overcame me in adolescence, I recall it as more a matter of a general mood, a mix of fear and melancholia, than of specific, clearly depressive thoughts. Decades later, when the illness received a clear diagnosis, I would understand the lived experience of my most depressive period as being connected to plot lines and motives that had great power over me. Much of what was alive in my mind could be loosely tied to that stew of the past, simmering along with recently added seasonings, such as professional success, arrogant behavior toward close family members, and an unhealthy number of fiercely held convictions.

After lengthy treatment—the most varied kinds of antidepressants and mood stabilizers, thirteen years in therapy—as well as all of the support from family that I received and continue to receive, when I do relapse, the experience is reminiscent of my teenage afternoons spent sleeping or my childhood fears. Today my depression returns without a specific plot, as a purely chemical reaction. More times than not, the old lady inexplicably sneaks up on me and robs me of my breath.

FIVE

VISIT TO THE CEMETERY

For decades, the subject of the siblings I lost or never had would show up in my life in various guises. As my parents' wordless melancholy or the backdrop to their separation. For a long time, it was above all a huge source of uncertainty that weighed over my solitary boyhood, as I realized that the majority of the boys and girls I knew had siblings. Unsure of the exact meaning of the word *fate*, I certainly questioned mine. Was some personal failing to blame for the fact that I did not deserve siblings? Still a child, without any notion of human reproduction, I had no way to understand the physical difficulties that kept my mother and father from having other children.

All of this swirled around my head or else could be sensed floating in the air. Naturally, I would later understand that they were unable to have children for reasons that eluded their control. The silence surrounding each miscarriage begat a family trauma that only grew the longer it went unmentioned.

The story I am telling now is the fruit of great reflection, but my father's shortcomings as a companion during those times my mother was recovering are recent news to me. In that era, husbands left pregnancy and the daily care of children almost entirely to their spouses. Beyond this, my father behaved more in the mold of a religious Jewish household in 1930s Hungary than in that of a secular marriage in 1950s Brazil. The injustice of the labor division between the couple had been even starker in the household in which André was raised, a far cry from what Mirta desired for her own married life. In any case, I was never able to hear my father's side of the story. I learned of his behavior from my mother only two years back, as we visited a cemetery.

On the whole, the household situation, complicated by the separation period and the continued loss of yet more dearly desired children, tainted the atmosphere at our house, placing enormous pressure on my shoulders. For as long as I can remember, I understood that my role was to be the principal source of joy for the rest of the family. My father would remind me that I should never forget that he was my best friend, and vice versa. He repeated this over and over, ad nauseam, while my mother stuffed me full of her doting and her anxieties. And so, at the center of my childhood, an almost pathological sense of responsibility began to bubble beneath the surface. I lived in constant fear of failing to please my parents.

Despite not liking to swim, I joined the swim team at the Clube Hebraica, since my parents, influenced by the erroneous opinion of a pediatrician, thought that I might never exceed my mother's own short stature, and that swimming would somehow help. I played all kinds of sports at the club, against my will and with only modest success, since my father forbade me to play the one I loved, soccer. I excelled in the goal, but André thought that the position of goalie would not contribute to my physical development. I cycled through swimming, basketball, judo, volleyball, but I was not allowed to play on the club's soccer team, where I would find true success and enjoyment, until after I turned thirteen. My protests against these obligations were pitiful, if in fact I even made them out loud.

Because I always spent school breaks alone, when I was

only five years old, my parents began to send me to overnight camps. These proved to be traumatic experiences.

At five, I went for the first time to Ma-Ru-Mi, a camp under the direction of individuals with German roots, in Campos do Jordão. I was the youngest camper, and I faced serious bullying. I would return for the next four years, never telling my parents what I went through. Ma-Ru-Mi had very strict rules. There were daily evaluations on the tidiness of our rooms, and we would all gather round to raise the camp flag soon after rising, the locale's frigid temperatures notwithstanding. During these rituals, we were punished for infractions in front of the other campers. The children were made to lie down and sleep following lunch, forbidden from leaving our rooms. One day, in bad need of the bathroom, I had to obey the camp counselor, who refused to let me get up. Filthy and wet, I had to clean the bed in front of the other children, thoroughly humiliated. To this day I ask myself whether I expressed the urgency of my situation or simply decided to quietly follow orders to a T. I became known as Pee Pants, a nickname that stuck as long as I would attend Ma-Ru-Mi.

On the way back to São Paulo at the end of each stay, as the bus pulled into the parking lot at Pacaembu

Stadium, where the parents were waiting for their children, I sat with my face glued to the window, trying to hide how miserable I'd been in Campos do Jordão and blocking out the parting insults directed my way. I tried to concentrate on what I would tell my parents. I generally told them only about the horseback riding, which in fact provided some of the few occasions I managed to leave the bullying behind as I galloped along. I don't know what other details I made up to paint a rosy picture of those days of torment at camp.

On the way back from one of these trips to Campos do Jordão, perhaps as a psychosomatic reaction to everything that happened or resulting from a sharp drop in immune resistance, I contracted four or five ailments in a row. I spent a month in bed. It all began with a nail fungus that had me soaking my feet in many a potassium permanganate bath prepared in the bidet. The bidet was transformed by that almost exotic bright purple, while my toes turned black and my toenails sloughed off. I spent hours a day looking at my feet, disappearing and reappearing in the lilac-colored solution, a macabre pastime. Some years ago, I wrote this scene into a short story, where a boy told the future by noting changes in the purple liquid in which he soaked his feet. It was a crude homage to Jorge Luis Borges. As I recalled those days spent with feet in the bidet, I remembered the narratives of the Argentine writer in which man's fate or the secret of the universe is connected to the stripes of a tiger, or to an Aleph in the cellar of some house. My story expressed a sort of veiled self-deprecation, in which I sought to make implicit that each of us has the Aleph we deserve. The fungus, if memory serves, was followed by the measles, mumps, and rubella.

During the last year I went to Ma-Ru-Mi, I recall the bittersweet experience of listening to the radio broadcast of Brazil's loss to Portugal in the 1966 World Cup in England. We all crowded together to listen to the game, which sealed our elimination from the Cup. There is always a strong sense of powerlessness when one's soccer team suffers a defeat. On the radio, this feeling is amplified. With twenty people between you and the dial, it only gets worse. Meanwhile, in the midst of my dejection, I became fascinated with the commentary, which the great Brazilian announcer Fiori Gigliotti began by declaring, "Curtains up, Brazil"; that was how he began the broadcast of every game. In his narration, the field became a carpet or deck, the Portuguese striker Eusébio a panther. Of course, I didn't know what a metaphor was, much less that in the future I would work to temper the use of such figures of speech. The dramatic effect with which Gigliotti narrated that defeat never left my mind. And I, having spent one more vacation in misery, listened in rapt attention as he declared at the end of the game, "It's all tears on the Brazilian side . . . It's all pain and suffering, ladies and gentlemen." From that moment on, I would prefer to go to games with a portable radio glued to my ear, listening to the voice of the great broadcaster.

When I was a bit older, I began to enjoy school vacations in São Paulo. At the age of nine or ten, I could take the bus by myself to the Clube Hebraica, where I would play soccer all day long, despite my father's order to practice my swimming. Before returning home on the same electric bus I'd come on, I would take a shower and wet my swimsuit, offering the soaked suit as evidence of the hours I had allegedly spent in the pool.

I would eat lunch alone at the club, which ended up being a lot of fun. I felt all grown up with menu in hand, seated at a poolside table in my sweaty soccer clothes. The offerings varied between two grilled cheeses on pita bread;

two kebabs with vinaigrette on a baguette; and the club's regular dishes, steak Diane with french fries or chicken Parmesan with white rice. At moments like these, I forgot to feel lonely.

On weekends, mustering some courage, I would offer my services as goalie to some older men. Despite being a runt, I was a standout on the pitch. I spent the days flying through the air as I nabbed the "bombs" they launched. During one of these games, a bystander who said he had trained on teams in Argentina picked me out to perform drills typically practiced by professional goaltenders. I think he must have been impressed by my performance and wanted to train me. We would practice on a separate field near the playground, where we did push-ups and other drills. I would snatch the balls he launched my way while he held my legs to the ground with his knee. Later, on my feet, I would jump, nonstop, from one side to the other of the improvised goalposts we made out of piles of jerseys or with empty soda bottles. At these moments, I forgot all other responsibilities beyond grabbing the ball and protecting the goal. I would leave exhausted and satisfied.

At the Colégio Rio Branco, I wasn't especially well liked by my classmates, because I could never shake off my anxiety over getting good grades. It was unthinkable to take a bad grade home or repeat my father's performance when he was a boy. And so, I became popular and made friends only when my gifts on the field were discovered. In middle school, my class made an unbeatable team. We won the intramural championship two years in a row. It was around that time when I and a few classmates were invited to represent the school in tournaments in the city and against other schools. My picture began to appear in the school newspaper, and many times, when gym class ran into the break, the other kids would crowd around to watch our squad play. I enjoyed performing my acrobatics, the same moves I had practiced so many times at the club or alone in our tiny apartment on Rua Itambé, kicking the ball against the wall, defending and narrating the entire thing with wild enthusiasm.

The downstairs neighbor complained about the constant bouncing of the ball against the wall and perhaps the play-by-play I practically hollered. For months, we waged battle between my ball and voice and the broom he used to hit the ceiling of his apartment and his angry cries for an end to the pandemonium. It was like a World Cup taking place in my bedroom all year long. Anytime my mother was sewing so that I couldn't play my games on the dining room table, the only other option I had in my free time was kicking that ball against the wall, for all the world to hear.

In my memory, soccer—whether the table or the wall-banging variety—and my trips to the Clube Hebraica appear as a brief cease-fire in my yearning for siblings. They belong to a period when I imagine I spent less time begging my parents for the gift I so badly wanted that never came. Perhaps I remember these things in such a compartmentalized way precisely because this was the period when my parents were supposedly their happiest. Before and after this interregnum, the sorrow and frustration at the children who never arrived, my father's inability to accept my mother's difficulty in carrying pregnancies to term, and their fights and gradual distancing made their way to me, even if they were never openly discussed. This created a situation in which my parents' only child longed for siblings to share his burden, which added to their own. None of this was done consciously, I'm sure, but today I am certain that it operated as one vicious cycle: they spiraled down, I asked for siblings, these siblings never came, they spiraled more, I asked for siblings . . .

———

ONE SATURDAY NIGHT ABOUT a year before I wrote this book, my mother watched a film in which the main character suffers a miscarriage. Every Sunday morning, I telephone and ask her about the previous evening's movie and festivities, time she always spends with Ruth, a childhood friend, whom she met at the time when, on the run from Yugoslavia, she lived in internment camps in Italy. That Sunday, my mother was so affected by the movie that she was unable to tell me about it by phone and asked me over for a talk instead. Face-to-face, she revealed that, after me, the only child who had made it to term, to whom my parents had given the name Rodolfo, was buried in the old Jewish cemetery in Vila Mariana, in an unmarked grave that she had never visited. My father had seen to the arrangements, as well as the birth and death certificates, and the circumcision, obligatory even for stillborn infants. Without it, the deceased child is not considered Jewish. Only then was he buried, while my father prayed the Kaddish, the prayer that Jewish people recite in the home during the week following the death of a family member, always at dusk. Mirta had not taken part in any of these rituals, and she wished all those years later to visit the cemetery. When Rodolfo was born, in 1958, I was a little older than two. I remember absolutely nothing of what I was told when my mother returned home without her belly or her child.

I had known only that I had one sibling who had been born, and he had been given this name. There were times when I even worried about him as if he had lived, imagining that with such an uncommon name he might have been bullied. I would transfer to Rodolfo what I underwent at camp or even, on a smaller scale, at school, because I was one of those students who never misbehaved in class or broke the rules.

TODAY, the cemetery in Vila Mariana is closed. To visit, one has to ask written permission. The Jewish community has grown significantly and has for a long time now buried its dead in a much larger space, far from the São Paulo city center, in the neighborhood of Butantã. The marker at Rodolfo's grave did not carry his name, or any date; it boasted only the number 18, nothing more.

The old cemetery is quite beautiful. The tombs are more of a piece, of the same size, in comparison with those in Butantã. For a long time, there was an unwritten rule among Jews never to distinguish among the dead according to their bank accounts. This has since been left behind, and so it's touching to see a cemetery with nearly identical tombs that still carry inscriptions in Hebrew.

It was extremely moving to visit with my mother the spot where my brother is buried, and to acknowledge his briefest of existences. Rodolfo lived only three days.

The failure to acknowledge the dead child, much like the all-pervading silence around the numerous attempts to have children, proved a much heavier burden than the truth that was never revealed. My parents, who sought in this case to protect me, hid even from themselves their failure to have "an entire soccer team of kids." This is how my mother describes her and my father's wishes at the time. "A soccer team" whose only player in the end was a goalkeeper. According to Mirta, my father married with no other intention than to have many children; love had nothing to do with it. That's not what André would tell me.

On the day of that first visit to Vila Mariana, my mother told me that the failed pregnancy preceding that of Rodolfo was particularly tragic, and contributed significantly to my parents' separation. As she remembers it, when the miscarriage began, André refused to accept the fact that his dream of having a second child was lost, and there was an ugly fight between him and my maternal grandmother, ultimately over whether my mother could receive the necessary medical attention. My father's relationship with my grandparents deteriorated greatly from that point on.

When I heard the detailed account, I empathized a great deal with my mother, but I couldn't manage to hate my father. Surely he would have his own version of events to share. However, sixty years had passed by the time I finally learned what took place that afternoon. With long gestation periods such as these, time and silence transform memory, construct narratives over the original narrative, and reopen old wounds, which grow in magnitude the deeper we bury their roots. There must be more than one version of what took place on that tragic day. But the others who were there can no longer speak, and a single truth remains, that which marked my mother for all the years of her life.

We decided to give Rodolfo a tombstone with a name and date, and a few months later we held a little dedication. On that day, it was his older brother Lajos—Luiz— who would pray the Kaddish for Rodolfo.

SIX

NICKNAMES

It is common in Brazil, and in my case with the added burden of being an only son and grandson, to call children by a diminutive form of their name from an early age—my parents, grandparents, and friends all do it to me. Perhaps their rush to protect me led them to infantilize me in several ways, including with my nickname. On the other hand, I was treated as a friend and confidant, which put me in a position more akin to that of a peer. There was something almost schizophrenic, or at least contradictory, in the way I was brought up.

My nickname stuck. It would be a thorn in my side for years. I didn't recognize myself as some defenseless child, and I assumed considerable responsibility before my time. My father sought in me a great friend, my mother a confidant, my grandfather a future peer or business partner, and my grandmother a stand-in son to spoil. All of them, meanwhile, united behind the diminutive, which to my ears had the ring of an insult.

At the Clube Húngaro, where we would go for lunch on Sundays before my father played cards, I was Luizinho, or Little Luiz. On vacations with a group of Hungarians to a lakeside beach called Praia Azul, the same thing. At my grandfather's printing business, where I spent some afternoons, ditto; that is why I preferred to go there on Sundays, when no one else was working. My grandfather was a workaholic. In this sense, during the early years of my own professional life, we were identical. To this day I can hear Giuseppe speaking with my voice, especially in lighthearted moments. Without thinking, I tell exactly the same sorts of jokes that he did. It's not uncommon for my wife, Lili, and Júlia, our daughter, to look over my way at such moments, as though looking at my grandfather.

On weekends, Giuseppe would take me to Cromocart and open the heavy iron accordion door, and spend the next two hours there, alone with his grandson. On such days, I wouldn't have to listen to the employees calling me by my nickname just to please my grandfather. I always found it odd the way I was treated at the printing business, where it was understood that I would be the future boss. Meanwhile, still in short pants, I was addressed in a way that perpetuated my status as child.

Perhaps now it's easier to understand my refusal of this role that was frozen in time, the child petrified by his nickname. At the time, it was merely one more weight upon my shoulders, a reinforcement of my position as son and grandson, as something essential to who I was. Sometimes, I asked them directly not to use the nickname; others, I just went along with it.

It was Luizinho who experienced bullying at the camps, and at school, or loneliness on afternoons when I waited to eat dinner with my parents. The bullying at school and my lack of friends would last for years, until two revolutions occurred in a brief span of time.

The first took place, as I've said, through soccer. I made a name for myself on my class team, complete with a photo of one of my great defensive efforts in the school newspaper, and was invited to join Rio Branco's school-wide team. This was one of the happiest moments of my teenage years: photographic evidence of a heroic save, wresting a ball from the corner of the net. I don't know how many times I've held that photo in my hands just to make sure the hero in the photograph was truly me. A short time before this, some of the strongest signs of the despondency on the horizon had begun to appear, and my parents had taken me to see a psychologist. After the silence and fear of my early years, this despondency and the desire to shut myself off by sleeping were the clearest signs that I suffered from depression or would soon.

The start of psychotherapy was great, but later I was transferred to group therapy, where I felt completely intimidated by others' sorrow and shared nothing. It was then that I was invited to play on the soccer and handball teams at Rio Branco. I wasted no time. I left my psychodrama behind and set off to keep balls out of the net. I would practice every night at school, except for Friday evenings and on weekends. Still, even then I found a way to practice on the school field, thanks to a janitor who would let me in, or else I practiced at the Clube Hebraica. At times, I was released from school to play in tournaments at other schools or clubs. Some of my happiest moments were at these tournaments. I played indoor soccer, field soccer, and handball at Rio Branco, all as a goalie. I was best at the first, though I also stood out in handball, a sport I didn't especially care for. I joined the recently formed team to help out the gym teacher, who had also invited me to join in other sports.

In indoor soccer, at first the starting spot in goal was occupied by a keeper for a team registered in the professional league. I served as honorary second-stringer. A year after I made the team, he went off to college, and I took his place. In handball, I played like a soccer goalie, leaping from one side to the other. But a ball thrown with the hands travels much faster than a kicked soccer ball. There isn't time to jump, and the goalkeepers tend to spend more time on their feet, moving their arms and legs to close off angles to the goal. Because it's quite difficult to defend the back of the net, the number of goals in a game is much higher. You have to have quick reflexes, especially when a ball bounces on the ground and comes back up at an odd angle. I would arrive at the game's end exhausted and with charley horses. It probably wasn't the most effective way to play, but it was what I was used to. During our soccer team's first tournament, we placed third, and I ended up catching the eye of a scout for a second-division professional soccer team, who invited me to a tryout. I was flattered, but I didn't even consider the offer. I didn't think I was that good at field soccer. Accepting that tryout was impossible given the degree of self-criticism I had developed at that stage.

THE SECOND REVOLUTION TOOK PLACE when I joined the Jewish youth movement at the Congregação Israelita Paulista, or CIP. At the age of twelve, I had already been to a summer camp run by the institution, where, for the first time, I was not bullied. There, I relaxed, participating in the music—I played guitar at the time—and the sporting games and competitions, where I performed well. Because I was a good student and a reader of books, I had success in a *College Bowl*–like quiz game, a test of general knowledge. The team that responded most quickly and correctly to questions from the camp counselors won the game. The CIP camp was also in Campos do Jordão, but utterly unlike my time at Ma-Ru-Mi, this was a soul-cleansing experience.

There were religious songs every morning and after meals—this last session being pretty informal. I felt so at home that I let my voice go. The music and songs of thanks for the food before us were useful for the melody and the ritual; no one bothered with the meaning of the prayers.

For a short time at camp, I earned a nickname that didn't bother me. I was known as Micheló, by virtue of a word that ought to be sung with a sharp jump in pitch that I used to showcase my ability to sing in tune. It was there in Campos do Jordão, at this bully-free camp, just before I turned thirteen, that I met my future wife, Lili. Four years later, she would become my lifelong companion.

Two years after that experience at camp, I joined a youth movement that could best be described as soft Zionism. Called Chazit Hanoar, it met out of a house next to the CIP synagogue, and hosted meet-ups among youth every Saturday afternoon, in addition to sponsoring camping trips, summer camps, and sporting tournaments with other Zionist groups, the majority of them based in the Bom Retiro neighborhood. The groups from this Jewish quarter of São Paulo were more fervently Zionist, while Chazit Hanoar was liberal and less strict when it came to religious education; in other words, it preached Zionism without much conviction. The middle-class families of the Jardins and Higienópolis neighborhoods wanted a certain proximity to Israel for their children, *pero no mucho*. Still, several of my friends from this period ended up moving there, after trips to harvest oranges or spending time in the kibbutzim. I never picked a single orange in my life, but I immersed myself in the work of Chazit as a counselor for the younger children, taking them to camps and discussing humanitarian or philosophical questions each week. I owe a great deal of my humanistic education and capacity to work in teams to this time.

The pro-Israel fanaticism or indoctrination never stuck with me, but the Jewish values did. I remember heated discussions with my father over Israel and its expansionist policy, conversations which took place, in general, during dinners after religious holidays—occasions when Jewish families do everything they can to pick a fight.

Even in the absence of any religious calling, I identify with Judaism and enjoy those rare moments I spend at temple, because it's there that I can feel my father again. Today I miss the sense of sadness that I experienced at seeing his eyes tear up. I would like to have done more for him. When André passed, I still attended the temple of my youth. His seat newly empty, I would stare the entire time at the spot where my father had most clearly expressed his despair and guilt. During the few hours that my son would come to stay by my side, I glimpsed a generational mirror game. Pedro is very much like me, and I in turn am very much like André. Gazing at his empty chair, or my son seated there, I would speak with André, on the High Holy Days. Today I still speak with him, at a different temple I've chosen to attend. Often I tell him of my sorrows and anxieties. I ask for his protection and help. I know that he has no power to change what happens here among us, but to ask him to be at my side feels essential. I try to imitate his timbre or his expression as I sing. I release my voice with great feeling, as though awash in pious fervor, just as he did. Imitating his voice is one of the things that makes me feel closer to my father. In a certain way, my song, too, is full of guilt, for having wanted to run out of temple so many times, though I did remain there at his request, if not exactly of my own accord. It is as if I am still atoning for each time I cast my eyes toward the mezzanine, for wanting to go talk to the other kids rather than understanding how much he needed me at his side at those moments when all he could think of was his own father. I also sing to release my guilt for having become exasperated at my inability to relieve his constant sorrow.

UNTIL I WAS SIXTEEN or seventeen, I could sing surprisingly in tune, just as my father had during the time he was a youth in the chorus at the Budapest opera house. I never managed to ask if this, at least, had brought my grandfather joy. After that age, I began to lose my pitch, though it was still better than my mother's; she most certainly was not born to be a musician. At temple, I make an effort to control my voice when it insists on slipping out of tune. I also try to match André's body language, grasping the book of prayer as I gaze ever so slightly toward the ceiling. On the few occasions that my children, and now my granddaughters, go to temple, I outdo myself during the musical portions, and I point out the moment's passage in the liturgy in the book of prayers. Exactly as he did when he noticed my mind wandering.

On the other hand, I am deeply irritated by all the other Jewish holidays outside the temple. The seder at

Pesach—with its long, repetitive conversation about the liberation of the Jews from slavery in Egypt—is for me the most boring night of the year.

My father was a faithful practitioner of the mitzvoth, acts of kindness, that are so crucial to Judaism. He would visit elderly Hungarian men and women at the Jewish hospital. At the reception area of the Hospital Albert Einstein, he would ask for a list of the patients and go up to the rooms of those who shared his nationality. At that time, this was still possible; currently such visits are performed only by rabbis. He paid for treatment for friends who only upon release were informed that their bill had been settled. For a time, he participated, just as my maternal grandfather had, on the board of the Lar dos Velhos, a senior home. He would lend money to fellow Hungarians, who many times left him high and dry. To this day, I remember the morning he learned that one of his best friends, a former partner in the clothier business, had taken advantage of him and fled to Israel. My mother poured out her rage on him, but he listened quietly before responding, "That's life."

Over the years, I often visited two of his closest friends who lived in the same senior home. I even lent money to one of them, like my father, without a thought as to whether I'd get it back. I always felt immensely happy when I walked into this friend's room and he told me that, for a second, he was sure it was André who had come to visit, the kindest man he ever met.

My father was that type of Jew, a temple-going Jew who performed acts of kindness. He took me to the religious service every Friday at sundown for many years, which was even worse torture for me. It was a more spartan ritual, lacking both the sorrow and the significance that the High Holy Days held for my father. The prayer on the eve of the day of rest is quite different from those that precede or take place on the Day of Atonement.

WITH MY PARTICIPATION IN CHAZIT, my personality underwent a total transformation. I went from a sad, quiet boy to a hyperactive type, the kind who asserts influence in collective endeavors with certain ease.

I didn't grow any closer to the religious side; I continued to sit uneasily next to my father at temple, but I also now represented the youth group on Jewish holidays, with homilies that employed metaphor and a heavy dose of adolescent philosophy. Rabbi Henry Sobel caught a glimpse of my sermons to the youth group and suggested to my parents that I would make a good rabbi. At one point I traveled to meet him, on an occasion when I was in Europe, and accompanied him to a conference in Belgium that included Golda Meir and Menachem Begin. The trip, however, was not enough to instill in me the desire to deepen my faith. At the time, I must have been seventeen, and it was incredible to be at the conference and shake Golda Meir's hand. I was a kid, tagging along with a half-crazy rabbi who liked my parents and thought I had a future in the faith. At the conference I did nothing other than listen quietly as great leaders engaged in bellicose discussions—as is common among us Jews—on various subjects, with a particular focus on the question of Israel's relations with the Arab world. As Golda Meir was much nicer than Menachem Begin, a right-wing Israeli leader at the time, I offered a lukewarm expression when shaking hands with the president of Likud. Beyond this, there I was once again being treated as older than my years, which must have stroked my ego, accustomed as it was to that sensation. I also recognize that, without my ever giving a thought to becoming a rabbi, standing there at the synagogue pulpit, reading my remarks rife with puerile poetic images, replete with hope for humanity, did a great deal for my morale, leaving me full of myself.

To this day, I couldn't tell you how the quiet, obedient, and sullen boy blossomed into a hyperactive youth with a knack for entertaining children. I became known as Luizão—Big Luiz—a nickname that came to me as spontaneously as its predecessor. I'm pretty sure this wasn't a result of my stature alone, but a mix of my height and my expansiveness and persuasiveness at Chazit. At the time, I sported denim overalls almost every day, with the Rolling Stones tongue sewed on the top part, plus red Converse All Stars, and wore my curly long hair in a style that we then called "black power." You would be hard-pressed to find this term used today to describe the hairstyle of a white upper-middle-class Jewish kid. Those were different times. This is the look that defined me during that time, the image of emancipation from a childhood full of diminutives.

In the youth movement, I also had moments of joy on the pitch, playing for the Chazit squad against our more Zionist rivals from Bom Retiro. I recall in vivid detail a save I made in a tournament played in the gymnasium of the Clube Hebraica among various Zionist youth organizations, a play similar to the one that made the Rio Branco newspaper: there I was, flying through the heavens and coming back down with the ball in my hands. The skyward gaze on my face that preceded both of these saves is of a different nature from that seen in the childhood photograph of me on my grandparents' sofa. In the photos of the goalkeeper, there is the palpable self-assurance of a boy who is sure he'll land with the ball firmly in his hands.

It was around this time that Lili and I again crossed paths. She attended the Colégio Objetivo, as did I, and we passed each other in the breaks between classes, but at Chazit I was in touch with her brother, who was my classmate, and her sister, who belonged to the group of younger kids I chaperoned. Though I had had two minor relationships before, it was with Lili that I learned what it is to love someone. We began to grow close again just before I turned seventeen. Despite my modest social success within the youth group, up to that point I had yet to come out of my shell in matters of the heart.

The sudden emergence of Luizão was not enough to

help me overcome my timidity in this area. My sexual initiation, at quite a young age, had taken place after my bar mitzvah with a prostitute procured by my father, and led to some serious hang-ups. I didn't really like the experience, but I repeated the ritual once a month for nearly two years, André always covering the tab. Soon thereafter I stopped going, certain that paying for sex was not something that brought me genuine pleasure. Curiously, in my visits to the "whores in private practice"—as my father called them—I would make appointments saying that it had been Simon, a bachelor friend of my father's, who had made the recommendation. I followed André's detailed instructions as to how to arrive at the location, introduce myself, and so on. Each time I left, my time up, the girl would always send her regards to "Uncle Simon" and smile. At a certain point, I came to suspect that the uncle in question was really my father. The first few times I returned from the red-light district, I found him waiting for me in the living room to ensure that everything had gone okay.

I believe that the last time I visited a prostitute was the occasion of a traumatic experience. It took place in a brothel on Rua da Consolação with a woman who had not been procured by my father. For starters, the result of that encounter was a case of gonorrhea, which had me taking painful injections of Benzetacil that left me limping home painfully the two blocks from the pharmacy.

The gonorrhea might well have given my father a certain sense of pride, but not me. Further, I recall that the girl began to refer to me in terms that infantilized me, along the lines of "Come here, little baby," the sound of which I found completely unbearable. I slapped a fistful of money down on a dresser and left the room in a rage, slamming the door on my way out.

My sex life became limited to the moments I locked myself in the bathroom, two or more times per day, to my father's chagrin. Though I couldn't tell you why, I chose just after lunch to hide away with magazines I would conceal in a newspaper. My father went so far as to knock on the door, perhaps out of some prejudice against masturbation, or else believing there was a danger I would settle for solitary sex. I suspect he also didn't like my reaction when, on a trip to Europe when I was thirteen or fourteen, we went to a belly dancing cabaret extravaganza, and I showed no enthusiasm when at one point a dancer sidled up to our table, shaking her breasts right under my nose. I remember I complained later that she had too much powder on her face. André couldn't understand my reservations on such occasions.

Between this time and my reencounter with Lili a few years later, I had only solo sex. I would buy men's magazines, as well as Carlos Zéfiro's unbelievable pornographic graphic novels, called "catechisms." Much more erotic than any photo could be.

One time, my parents traveled to Holland and came back telling all their friends about De Wallen, the red-light district where the prostitutes were exposed in windows. At the country club we often visited in Atibaia, there were whispers that a magazine with explicit sex scenes was making the rounds. At the time, no one had seen such a magazine, showing couples screwing in detail, as though they were photo-novels without subtitles, in full-page color spreads. The close-ups on the female sexual organ were so realistic that when I finally saw them I was astonished, even though I was not a virgin. It was like a porn movie today, in magazine form. It caused a huge uproar at the club, whose members were largely middle-class Jews like my parents.

Imagine my surprise when I discovered that the person

who had brought said magazine to the country club was my father. It was a gem of sexual liberation, and made its way among the older boys but was forbidden to me. Only after months of arguing was I allowed to flip the pages.

My father developed something of a reputation for his playboy-ish, voyeuristic behavior, par for the course among the Clube Húngaro set and the friends he went with to the Clube Hebraica sauna every Wednesday night. André was not the kind of man to have many extramarital affairs. According to my mother, he received no small amount of attention from several women at the club. However, as a matter of principle, he was opposed to serious sexual or romantic adventures out of wedlock. But he enjoyed his cards, his parties, his crooning, and considered red-light escapades part of a married man's life. On one occasion, when he erroneously suspected that my marriage to Lili was on the rocks, he called me aside. He preferred to discuss matters on a stroll through the streets, as night was falling. He told me he had sensed that something was afoot in our relationship, and he wished to give me an important bit of advice. After fumbling for words, he told me that if one day I felt any sort of physical need not satisfied in my marriage, I ought never to become seriously involved with another woman, but rather seek out a "professional."

He scared me half to death, not least because there was no reason for him to be worried about my marriage at the time. Moreover, I was more than positive that I would never call upon the services of a prostitute. I never told my father that I hadn't enjoyed my experiences; he wouldn't have understood. I walked back home with my hand on André's shoulders, and I gently thanked him for his advice, which he had offered in his clumsy way with words strewn with grammatical errors and the thick accent he never lost.

At that exact moment, I remembered another stroll I had taken with my father, also at nightfall, when we still lived on Rua Itambé and I was nine. He had called me aside after dinner and said he wanted to take a walk with me. We headed down our street toward Rua Major Sertório, in the red-light district, locale of the higher-end nightclubs, like the famous La Licorne. I had walked that same path many times, because a bit farther down the street was the store where I would take my slot car collection to be fixed. I'm fairly certain that, up until that point, I hadn't taken note of the legendary club, or else

I hadn't understood what exactly went on there. When we made it to the front door, André asked me if I knew what the place was, and then gave me the first lessons in my sexual education. He felt a certain pride at showing me the man's life, and told me that after my bar mitzvah I could either visit the brothels or else visit a prostitute "in private practice." It's a bit puzzling that, as he gave me sex advice, the example he used was La Licorne and not that of a man and woman making love. On such strolls, not to mention Sundays when we would set out to watch pickup soccer matches or follow the acrobatics of model airplane pilots with their tiny planes in Ibirapuera Park, he would return to his old refrain: We were each other's best friend. We would take the car down Avenida Rubem Berta and stop at the amateur soccer fields on either side, beneath the dirt banks along the route to the Aeroporto de Congonhas. We squatted down, hugging our knees with our hands to keep ourselves upright. The teams captivated me with their colorful uniforms and I would visualize myself tending goal for one or the other. The fields were beaten earth, almost red in tone. As we squatted, he would repeat: "Never forget, I'm your best friend, and you're mine." It was like renewing a blood pact. He and I believed in this. But his insistence weighed on me.

Years later, I also stopped tagging along when the young men my age at the country club in Atibaia set out for the night life, "on the prowl for women." I didn't think of myself as capable of "sweet talk," picking out a girl, then trying to talk her into a quickie in the back seat of my parents' car. We were still underage, but parents generally pretended, with a certain sense of pride, to look the other way when they handed over the keys so their sixteen-year-old sons could go "nab a girl" in the city. I was a total zero in this department. I didn't even try. Once, I went to a Carnival dance, but I was a terrific failure, and soon thereafter was saved by my reencounter with Lili, who became my girlfriend, freeing me once and for all of the "obligations" of a young Jewish Don Juan or playboy.

It was a great thing to learn about love and sex at nearly the same time; in light of my long love affair, I don't count my trips to the brothel and "whores in private practice" as learning experiences at all.

This era of wild saves at goal, the end of my psychodrama, my social success in the Jewish group, and my reunion with Lili brought another Luiz to the fore: assertive, possessing a certain leadership capacity, and increasingly sure of himself. Periods of melancholy became rarer, though they never ceased. My success on the college entrance exam and, later, in my early career saw the pendulum swing to one side—the Luizão side. Each passing day brought a certain radical growth in my perfectionist personality, mixed in with vestiges of melancholic tendencies. This abundance of confidence that has characterized my life since then, at Chazit, at university, in my first job, would be responsible for making me the publishing professional that I would become over time; but it would also give birth to a bipolar personality that had not appeared during my childhood or else hadn't been identified. Today I am certain that my two nicknames signal a rupture in my personality, which would reach extremes. The price paid—by me and my entire family—was steep.

SEVEN

BEETHOVEN

It's difficult to pin down the beginning of the almost gruesome obsessiveness that defined my entry into adulthood and the work world. At a certain point, I ceased to be merely a son seeking his parents' approval with good grades, obedience, and submissiveness, and I started to apply ideals of perfection to certain tasks, often with uncommon determination. Later, this new personality trait would mingle with a growing taste for the arts, particularly literature and music, and a penchant for collecting.

My mother was the one in my family who nurtured these interests. Without work beyond her domestic chores—at least after she abandoned her home-based sewing business—she read intensely, sending books off after reading to be bound in leather, with marbled paper. When they came back from the binder, I would stand

and admire them alongside her. They were beautiful. Taking them in our hands and placing them back on the shelf was a thrill we shared.

Accompanying Mirta, I, too, would visit bookshops that procured books from abroad via special order. These stores were located in shopping arcades in the city center and imported all the latest titles, from bestsellers to more literary texts. That was where she would acquire the novels that she read in between the classics of world literature. Some of these books she would later buy in Portuguese and urge me to read: *Exodus* by Leon Uris, *The Godfather* by Mario Puzo, *Airport* by Arthur Hailey, and *It Can't Always Be Caviar* by J. M. Simmel, among so many others. I read these books at quite a young age. My mother had a modest collection of Brazilian writers. Beyond Jorge Amado, her favorites were Érico Veríssimo and Graciliano Ramos. She was also a fan of more popular writers, like Sra. Leandro Dupré, who was all the rage among my mother's generation of women. Thanks to Mirta, I devoured Amado's *Tent of Miracles* when I was still a young boy. As a result, it became my favorite book by the great writer from Bahia.

As I wrote earlier, I read my first children's encyclopedia at the foot of my mother's bed, for months on end, and also received my first reading recommendations from her, with special consideration for Charles Dickens and his youthful tragedies, which had a huge impact on me. I must have read *Oliver Twist* at a very young age, and I identified with the poor orphan boy. That whole situation was much worse than not having siblings. Despite the strong connection I felt to my father as a young boy, my professional calling was born at my mother's side—during her plodding convalescences, during our visits to bookshops, and in the act of taking the books she'd so passionately had bound into our hands, savoring a whiff of their pages.

During the month of various illnesses set off by Ma-Ru-Mi, I read nonstop. I must have been eight or nine, and I read some children's novels, and even some of the more accessible adult books, and devoured the Tintin comics. It was during this period that my father recommended a book to me, for the first and only time. One afternoon after lunch, he walked into my room with a pocket edition. The novel, written by Ferenc Molnár, was titled *The Paul Street Boys*. André tossed the cheap little volume on my lap and told me it was his favorite book. At first glance, I thought it was a cartoon strip, but what really caught my attention was the fact that my father had gone to a bookshop especially for me. I wasn't sure how to react; I wasn't expecting him to suggest a book to me. On account of his recommendation and its moving chronicle of childhood heroism, it is perhaps the book that has had the greatest impact on my life. The plot revolves around the battle over a *grund*, an empty lot coveted by two groups of boys. I really related to the bravery of Nemecsek, the smallest member of the group protecting the *grund* against attack. I had been confined to bed for some time, and I would have loved to be considered a hero and not merely the youngest of the bunch, as I had been that first year at Ma-Ru-Mi, leading to an enduring personal tragedy. I longed to become a Nemecsek and transform from runt to giant. With his death from pneumonia and through his acts of heroism in the defense of the *grund*, Nemecsek is remembered for all time; he receives deathbed plaudits from friends and adversaries alike and becomes the protagonist of a book! What more could I want after yet another unfortunate summer camp? With *The Paul Street Boys*, it was as if I had finally stepped out onto the empty lot next to my building, while in fact I only stared down from the upper floors.

In the world of the arts, my father stuck with opera; it was an artistic form he could relate to, much more so than the literature or visual arts that formed my mother's mindset. He would take me to the Theatro Municipal in São Paulo on Sundays for matinee performances. The sets were a tad pathetic, especially in the eyes of a boy under ten. One afternoon, when we were to go watch *Il Guarany*, one of the few famous Brazilian operas, I couldn't stand it anymore and lifted the thermometer to the bedroom lamp to fake a fever. I think my childish attachment to realism was warning me that those super-white singers, with their protruding bellies and wigs, wouldn't fare well in the skin of Don Antonio's beautiful daughter Ceci and the handsome, young indigenous man Peri. The matinees at the Municipal to which I was introduced compulsorily and precociously ought to have been sufficient to completely turn me off to the opera. I haven't the slightest idea how this didn't come to pass. On the contrary, today opera is one of my greatest passions.

Perhaps the lifelong miracle that music has been for me came from an unexpected gift from my father. It was a Saturday, and we were on a visit to a stationery shop in

Bom Retiro that sold Cromocart greeting cards. While André went to speak with the owner, I found, in the back of the shop, a small section of LPs, and I became obsessed with one of them: the Beatles' *A Hard Day's Night*. I believe it was the four Liverpool boys and their haircuts that sucked me in. It's conceivable that I had heard something about them, or seen a cover band—the Beatles, the name spelled with two *e*'s—play their music on RecordTV. This was in 1964 or 1965, I was eight or nine years old, and that was my first LP.

I couldn't get enough of that album, and I made my father take me with him on more visits to the stationery shop for more gifts like that one. I remember getting *Beatles for Sale* and *Help!* soon after those albums made it to Brazil. But these might well have been presents from my grandmother, who made my musical interests her own. With the clear aim of spoiling me without my parents' knowledge, Mici would take me to various stationery shops, and later give me an allowance especially for LPs.

Sometime later, I subscribed to rock magazines, *Rolling Stone* and *Cash Box*, the latter only to keep up with the record charts. It was not enough to just know what was popular or listen to music on lunch-counter juke-boxes. I had to have every album that made it to the top of the list; I had to listen to every kind of rock there was, buying imported albums at certain specialty stores.

At age eleven, I was a regular at the stores that sold imported records, all thanks to the support of the Mici Weiss Foundation. My grandmother provided me with a true family slush fund for indulging my taste for music. Later on, it was she who bought me my sound systems. Every birthday, we would go to the Raul Duarte audio and video store on Rua Sete de Abril. I wanted to hide at the sight of that energetic little woman fiercely bargaining with the store owner, who was always very kind and patient. To her mind, making a purchase without negotiating was no fun, or perhaps this bargaining assuaged her guilt. My grandparents were in a good financial situation, but they didn't permit themselves any luxuries, with the exception of those Mici showered on her grandson. At first, I nearly died of shame, then of joy, as she gave me new speakers, amplifiers, reel-to-reel tape recorders, and CD players, which got better from one year to the next.

My parents, aware that one wrong turn was one too many for an only child, never bought me anything over-the-top, but they looked the other way when it came to my grandmother's spoiling me. Perhaps they enjoyed seeing me so entranced by music.

Before the more sophisticated models, I had in my room a tiny plastic record player to listen to 45s, the ones with a large hole in the middle. The one that impacted me the most was a recording of "My Way," which had climbed back to the top of the charts in the voice of Brook Benton, a soul artist. I wasn't familiar with the Frank Sinatra version and I didn't care to be at that time. But I sang "My Way," to a soul beat, nonstop. Later, when I heard the Sinatra recording, I completely dismissed it. For me, "My Way" was Black music. Over time, my father incorporated the Sinatra version into his own singing repertoire, which generally consisted of Hungarian Romani music or famous opera arias. But it was as though we were singing different songs. Each of us had his own "My Way."

At a time when I had yet to receive the record players for LPs, I would listen to music in the living room in the afternoon. Sometimes at lunch, I was given permission to listen to one of my albums with my parents, as long as it wasn't heavy metal and I kept the volume low. That was when I played the record "Je t'aime . . . moi non plus," a wild success in dance halls and on the charts. I was thirteen, and I might have already been with Nina, the first prostitute my father had arranged. But, either due to distraction or because Nina was terrible at feigning a moan, I didn't catch on that Jane Birkin and Serge Gainsbourg were imitating a sex act as they sang. To my ear, the song was sensual but not explicit. My parents' cheeks turned red; they smiled but asked me to put a different album on.

I can remember listening to music for hours on end, waiting for my magazines to arrive while dreaming of the next acquisition. From rock, I moved on to jazz and then Brazilian pop. Sometime later, I began to buy classical music albums. Perhaps the first was the soundtrack of *Zardoz*, a Sean Connery sci-fi film. Beethoven's Seventh Symphony, which appears on the soundtrack, caught my attention when I was seventeen and remains my favorite symphony.

For every kind of music that existed, I had to have everything, know everything, scrutinize everything. A manic-obsessive temperament was slowly being constructed, via one of the best tools: music.

As I delved more deeply into classical music, I read all the guides that came into my hands. I was already older at this point and the obsessive component of my personality was considerably more accentuated. I ran a highlighter over all the recommendations in the books and bought them one by one. There were hundreds.

Later, I began to research the best recordings; I was in search of the sublime, the most perfect form of expression to be found among all the concertos, sonatas, and symphonies. As the years passed, I set out to acquire several copies of works I already had by the boatload, in an attempt to discover which version was closest to perfection. Plenty of musical aficionados do the same. They are always in search of a new interpretation of their favorite pieces. What differs is the degree of obsession, and the role this incessant search takes in their lives. No doubt I am among the more fanatical. This personality trait, which emerged in late adolescence, would become important to understanding the obstinance I would show in my dedication to books and the work of a publisher.

I listen to music nearly all the time. It's a bad sign when I can't find anything I like. It means I am immersed in a kind of absolute silence and at a point where not even music can reach me. Still, this is the way, starting with that first trip to Bom Retiro and especially thanks to my grandmother, I ended up a collector of albums, and came to use the purchase of albums, and years later this search for ever more interpretations, as an antidote to periods of melancholy or boredom.

The act of collecting has a maniacal, perfectionist aspect to it, and tends to develop in people who feel a need to always be in search of an ideal, a flood of emotions, or the thrill of acquisition. In my case, it fills a recurring gap.

For those with serious bipolar disorder, spending money can quickly get out of control. They buy refrigerators or cars they have nowhere to put. Though I was belatedly diagnosed with bipolar disorder, I never reached that point. However, I recognize that certain habits of mine related to music and the arts have had both a positive side and a side that speaks to some deep personal weaknesses. My repeated and heavy consumption of albums, the compulsion to attend memorable concerts that takes over before I go on a trip, or my desire to own certain artworks and to stare at them in search of something singular are harmless forms of dealing with a sadness that reaches to the depths of my soul, independently of how my life might be going at the moment.

I am aware that I was raised in a family and personal environment that permitted such luxuries, hardly essential to a happy life, despite the maniacal value they've taken on for me personally.

The social conscience I acquired over the years, in particular during the period of student struggle against the military dictatorship, has not been enough to entirely eliminate my collector's manias. It's true that when I was involved in the student movement and marches, my collecting tended more toward opposition and alternative newspapers than albums. I subscribed to the main left-wing publications, which drove my parents crazy. They worried that the building superintendent or the doorman would report me to the police. So I began to buy what were called "dwarf newspapers" from the newspaper stands. At times, I worked myself into such a frenzy anytime a new publication came out that I would act just as I had with albums: I would go to the newsstand every day to see if the latest issue had been released.

I also bought an absurd number of Marxist and anarchist books. As voracious a reader as I was, I never made it through that mountain of pages. I was a regular at all the bookstores that carried left-wing books. Worried sick, my parents told me the police would photograph visitors to Livraria Ler from the Colégio Caetano de Campos. This only whipped me up into a further frenzy, and I began to visit more often. Shortly before university, in a hyperpolitical phase, I set novels aside. I would go camping with Lili and take along only the most difficult writers. I almost never set foot in the sea, instead reading Gramsci, Lukács, or Bourdieu, ensconced in the shade of our beach tent. It goes without saying that I was unable to fully recognize that my revolutionary impetus was accompanied by personal habits that were more than bourgeois. I acted as if the sun and sea were counter-revolutionary.

Ever since receiving those first gifts from my father and my grandmother, I had filled my head with dreams of acquiring this or that, with a desire, always tied to some distant future, that might take form through the most disparate combinations of possessions: LPs, books, newspapers, concerts, paintings . . .

During a particular period, even soccer would get wrapped up in my collector's compulsion. At first with cards and table soccer squads, later with goalkeeper gloves that I asked my grandmother to bring back from her trips to Europe. She would travel with my grandfather to international conferences in Frankfurt and bring back professional goalie gear. When I first began to play, not a single goalkeeper wore gloves. The trend began with the 1970 World Cup, when Gordon Banks, the English keeper, and Félix, on the Brazilian side, began to use them. The Brazilian's goalie gloves looked to be your average leather gloves. I dreamed of those things. I read about the best kinds, and about the different brands the most famous players used. Once again, my grandmother made an appearance, and soon I was sporting not just flashy tennis shoes but imported gloves to play indoor soccer. The glove that's made for the outdoor game isn't always ideal for indoors. But as a collector's item, it seemed essential to me from the start. What's more, all my vanity was channeled into goalkeeper uniforms, especially gloves. I was more concerned with my sporting outfits than with my everyday clothes. Arriving home from a game, I would wash the gloves, check for any tears in the rubber lining, and then stow them in a special drawer, as though they were precious stones or antique watches.

PEOPLE LIKE ME WHO DEVELOP an outsize sense of responsibility for others shouldn't tend goal. One bad play can cause irreparable damage to a team. A goal from the other team would send me into despair in seconds. I would rewind the shot over and over in my mind, as though it were a film, teasing out the particulars of my failure. I longed to turn back time, to retell the story, with a spectacular save. Similarly, my constant soccer playing into my forties—when my playing declined and I abandoned the pitch once and for all—held great importance for me. Lili used to say she knew whether I had won or lost my night games or Saturday-afternoon matches by the way I closed the door when I arrived home.

Collecting great saves was less expensive than collecting LPs or books. There were greater risks involved, but when I played well, it was wonderful. When I was saving my team in the goal, I returned to the happiest parts of my childhood and adolescence. On the pitch, I found my original source of redemption.

Today, in the absence of soccer, I often let music speak for me. I do this nearly every day. Choosing what to listen to is like picking out someone to speak on my behalf, or someone to talk to. That's why periods when the music stops are worrying. From an early age, I learned to live without ever saying how I felt. Over time, I came to attribute an almost negative quality to words: If I needed to explain what I was thinking it was because no one understood me. Or else words could never faithfully represent my feelings. The Paulinho da Viola track that speaks of "a samba [. . .] without melody or words / so as not to lose its meaning" became a personal anthem, though I had always believed up to that point that melody was crucial. A samba without words: this was the purest form of expression. My favorite writers never narrate in excess; they make the most of what is left unsaid. I especially admire those whose writing is peppered with many silences—Thomas Bernhard, Albert Camus, W. G. Sebald, Machado de Assis, and Jorge Luis Borges. I prefer short stories above all for this same reason. In the case of stories, what is left out is as important as what is left in, perhaps even more so.

I would never discuss my feelings with my parents. Or, if I did, I would conceal any trace of sadness or discontent. At the beginning of my relationship with Lili, she had a hard time with my silences. I wanted her to understand everything without my having to explain. Misunderstandings led to silence and never to conversation. She had to guess at what was going on with me; after all, this was the proof of a great love affair.

One of the books that would impact me in adulthood was Oliver Sacks's *Seeing Voices*, in which the renowned neurologist and writer takes on the richness of sign language and the many nonverbal forms of expression used by deaf people or by those who were not trained to use spoken language. In this book I came into contact with the case of wild boys put on display in Europe as exotic royal objects, and with the true story of the sailor who spent four years alone on an island and inspired Daniel Defoe's *Robinson Crusoe*. Surrounded only by nature, the real-life castaway succumbs to the natural world and loses his use of verbal language. The true story is the opposite of Defoe's fable, where a man obtains complete dominion over the forest and domesticates wild animals. When he was found, the Scottish sailor Alexander Selkirk had to relearn how to speak.

Under the influence of my appreciation for silence, and trying to write a novel after my short story collection *Discourse on Some Blades of Grass*, I tried to construct a narrative of all the stories I researched about the subject after reading Sacks's book. I covered ground ranging from Victor of Aveyron to Kaspar Hauser, and on through literary characters like Mowgli and Robinson Crusoe. I wrote long passages on details of Jonathan Swift's *Gulliver's Travels*, and about little-known stories by Daniel Defoe. I also spent pages on a mad Austrian sculptor, a follower of Mesmer, named Franz Xaver Messerschmidt. I had seen his sculptures in a museum in Vienna and never forgot them. Messerschmidt made sixty alabaster busts representing forceful facial expressions that no human being could ever intentionally reproduce. The sculptures correspond to the full range of human expression, without using a single word.

I finished the novel, but the result was awful. It had too many ideas and not the least bit of coherence as fiction. Three editors at Companhia das Letras at the time,

Maria Emília Bender, Marta Garcia, and Heloisa Jahn, were frank and helped me to put that ill-fated venture to rest. After some time, I managed to remold the novel into just four pieces that, alongside others, appeared as a collection. Basically, the story they tell is of an unidentified narrator who marries Antônia, a teacher who delivers lectures to deaf students using sign language and tells the stories of Beethoven and Goya, among others, during each class. Antônia had in fact been renamed as homage to the woman to whom Beethoven wrote a famous letter, in which he referred to the recipient as his "immortal beloved" without ever having had an affair with her, or with any other woman, for that matter. The stories have fewer defects than the novel, and are only part of this narrative to show how spontaneous nonverbal expression has always been important to me, something that I continue to hold up as an ideal. Antônia's husband never says what he is thinking. And she holds forth throughout—in sign language. It was this form of communication that gave name to the collection. When I was a child, I never opened up, much less sought to be understood or have company, having little need to talk with anyone. On the soccer pitch, I had no need for words, other than in those moments when I would warn my teammates about some imminent scoring threat, which I did loud and clear. Though part of a team, I repeated in the goal a type of solitude I knew well. In my love life, I reached the place I wanted to be quite early, giving a good deal of work to Lili but freed of the need to explain myself much. There have been moments when I've spoken at length, in general during manic episodes or when on an ego trip. However, silence and music have almost always been essential for me. During periods when I wasn't properly medicated, I began to act quite differently from the way I do today, talking more than I should, seeking attention. I grew tired of having to be gently warned by Lili on such occasions. This no longer happens, and I can't stand to remember the times I was capable of such unseemly logorrhea.

Now much older, I wake up in the middle of the night, once or twice, and can hear a song playing within. From time to time, this even makes it difficult to fall back asleep. There's no rhyme or reason to what is playing, somewhere between slumber and wakefulness. It might be a top hit from forty years ago, from the time of my plastic record player, or a song I heard recently on the radio or even in the shower the morning prior. While writing this book, however, when I wake up and there's still no sign of light creeping through the windows, it is practically only Beethoven's symphonies or piano sonatas that play in my head.

And so, for many years now I've been living in a world of few words, in an ambiguous silence. It can be as soothing as it is oppressive and addictive. In this vacuum, my manias create alternate realities, always much more imaginary than concrete. From an early age, I began to live in the future, my mind turned toward the next album I would buy, the next goal I would save, and, when I was a little boy, visualizing the next car that would turn at the street corner where I lived, whose make I tried to guess. To this day, it's rare that my mind is capable of living in the present, because the present has no room for perfection. Of course, neither perfection nor lasting experiences of the sublime are to be found in the days yet to come, either. But the future is always more accepting of our illusions.

EIGHT

THE SILENCE AND FURY

Obedience and silence have been constants during much of my life. In childhood and adolescence, it was taking care not to displease my parents that counted most. Throughout the years, these two components gradually ceased to play equal roles; the excessive obedience I showed my parents would disappear forever, but the silence, on the contrary, would only increase. During the time when I was surrounded by friends from my Jewish youth group, I would share secrets and utopian visions for the world, and I led a bustling social life. In terms of love, it was important that I found Lili at such an early age. For someone with a personality like mine, the ups and downs of relationships would be even more difficult or painful to handle.

Over time, I would increasingly return to the silence

that ruled my childhood. In this sense, my horizons would gradually shrink until they included only my closest family. In the international world of publishing, I have many friends, but something pushed me to avoid the nights out, the dinners, and the hype at book fairs. I'm not sure how to explain this behavior. The arrogance I developed when I first tasted professional success played a role in the most serious depressive episode I've had. The fear of another collapse, like the one that hit me at the age of forty-three, increasingly led me to shut myself off from others.

I would monitor myself for the slightest sign of vanity, which isn't always a detrimental force in our lives. Attending the parties at book fairs tends to accentuate a kind of narcissism: you see yourself in those who praise and woo you; it can be fun, intoxicating even, but for someone who has been through what I have, the risks are just too great.

I had a huge ego trip after my success as an editor at Brasiliense publishing house, and another, not quite as serious, in the early years of Companhia das Letras. During the first, I was twenty-two; during the second, thirty.

I hope to have stopped in time. After the depressive episodes following my professional success, silence and solitude increasingly seemed like less dangerous alternatives.

Having chosen that path, I again began to feel considerable shyness in social situations. I'm still terrified by parties with seating plans, but I am also petrified of having to sit next to someone who isn't part of my most intimate circle. When the choice is left to me, I become paralyzed and can't decide whom to sit next to. Asking if someone would like to join me, or whether a certain seat is free, is a cause of considerable anxiety. At receptions for authors at my house, rarer and rarer these days, I roam the room like a zombie, and when it's all over I ask Lili who came and what they talked about.

I manage to provide the necessary leadership at work, but most of the time, socially, I'm something of a hermit.

Before silence came to define my personality, I underwent a long period of hyperactivity, both at Brasiliense and at Companhia das Letras. Books and success had me constantly buzzing. The day we published Fernando Morais's *Chatô, o rei do Brasil*, a biography of Brazilian media mogul Assis Chateaubriand, I ended up at the doctor, my blood pressure sky-high.

The first signs I was losing control appeared during the Luizão period, in my parents' house, especially during quarrels with Mirta. I became enraged for lesser reasons, too, such as a record player that insisted on stopping before it reached the last track or a swivel chair that fell apart. I broke my sound system with a karate chop, and I shattered my bedroom window with a bicycle kick after an argument with my mother on the eve of my wedding. At the sound, she immediately worried that I had thrown myself out the window. The chair, I destroyed in a flurry of kicking and stomping. On another occasion, after I was married, I took a cane to the roofing insulation of our house after learning that my secretary had failed to pay the monthly health insurance premium at a time when I had just come back from surgery on my leg. A number of times I punched the wall after family disagreements, and once destroyed a poster with a right uppercut to the nose of one of Picasso's muses. At such moments, the feeling of not being able to control myself was unbearable.

In elementary school, I once locked horns with a

classmate, but on several other occasions I reacted with silence or resorted to strategies to remove myself from potential confrontations, especially if there was no way for me to take on a large group of boys.

I can remember an incident when, around the age of four, I was attacked by an older boy in the Praça Buenos Aires and ran home crying. My father took me to his room and asked what had happened. When I told him that I'd been punched in the face and hadn't fought back, André asked me where I was hit, and then smacked me on the other side of the face. It was, he said, for me to learn to never leave insults unanswered.

On one of numerous occasions when my father denied my request to join the soccer team at Hebraica, he enrolled me in judo classes. I had already tried swimming, volleyball, and basketball, quickly growing impatient with the meager results of my efforts at these sports. The judo academy was located at the tail end of Avenida Angélica; I could walk there from my house, and as a bonus, I could grab a hamburger at one of the newfangled neighborhood lunch counters on my way back, where everything was a novelty: the famous jukebox where we could play records of top hits, the unreal bacon and egg hamburgers, frappés, sundaes, yellow cows (ice cream floats made with Guaraná soda) or black cows (Coca-Cola floats)—these treats nearly made up for the work of judo training when I'd rather be snatching goals out of the air.

In the struggle in which I was engaged, I needed to satisfy my father's orders. I had neither talent nor interest in judo, and yet, soon after I began to train, I was called up for a competition. It was a huge meet of all the Yamazaki academies, in the gymnasium at Pacaembu Stadium. The event opened with a curious spectacle: hundreds of children in profile, donning white kimonos, ready to compete. I was a white belt, the lowest rank, but I went imbued with the mission to perform well. Given how little I'd trained, I had little to no technique, but I could not fail. My father was in the bleachers. I won all four matches. Unsure how to execute a range of blows, I held my adversaries' kimonos firmly and refused to allow them to land a single strike.

In addition, I shoved my opponents to the edge of the mat, simulating blows I hardly knew how to execute. I won some of the matches by *waza-ari* (an imperfect hit worth a half point) and others merely for my combativeness, which is used as a tiebreaker. I won not a single victory by *ippon*, the fatal blow. Undefeated, I placed first in my group, and I skipped straight from white belt to purple, a color that reminded me of the traumatic nail fungus I contracted at Ma-Ru-Mi but nonetheless filled me with pride. It goes without saying that my father was radiant as we left Pacaembu. In his eyes, from the punch in Praça Buenos Aires to the purple belt in judo, important progress had been made.

The trauma of the war in which Jews were unable, or unsure how, to react, remained ingrained for several generations. The willingness to fight that my father recognized on the mat must have held meaning beyond the medal I earned. It might have brought him back to the moment when he and my grandfather confronted Hungarian Nazi militias. On that occasion, which would have such tragic consequences, András and Lajos were one.

In basketball, one event shows how focused I was in moments that demanded accountability. I never made the starting squad at Hebraica. I didn't care for the sport; I was there because my father demanded it—as if shooting the basketball would make me shoot up in height. I was the sixth man on the team, first among reserves. One afternoon, when a visiting team came to play in our gymnasium, I spent nearly the entire game on the bench. In the final minutes, I was sent in to shoot two free throws. I wasn't quite sure why I was put on the court at such a decisive moment, because there were five players on the team who were better than I was. The coach understood that I wasn't one to dodge responsibility and sent me in at that crucial juncture. The Hebraica team won the contest by two points, after I made both shots just as the game was ending.

Years after the judo tournament, my inability to gauge my own strength came back to bite my father. The setting was the country club in Atibaia, and after some joke or other he and I locked horns at the edge of the pool. We were just horsing around, nothing serious, but I lost control and landed a *koshi guruma*, a blow from my judo days. A former boxer much stronger than I was, my father flew over my back and fell on the ground. Because he hadn't been expecting it and didn't know how to fall properly, something we'd learned at the academy, my father was furious. His face turned completely red and, humiliated, he left the pool. I surveyed the scene and noticed that most of the people around us were looking on without understanding a thing. I tried to make my apologies, but these would not be accepted until days later. There was no conscious motive for such violence; I don't believe it amounts to an Oedipal moment, or that I was exacting some sort of revenge for the way he sometimes subjected my mother—and, from a young age, my ears—to shouting. I must have misjudged my strength or wanted to show off for André, after so many years. Or I lost control and landed a blow on the wrong person in the wrong place. There was Luizão, in full force.

A few violent outbursts might have been echoes of that blow I received on the street. In other cases, I ask whether these were signs of the bipolar disorder I would develop. Some say it must have been a simple angry reaction, same as anybody has. Nonetheless, those who are bipolar sense precisely when the situation is getting out of control, and are familiar with the regret and guilt that flood our heads, in an attempt to completely erase what just happened. Both moments—the rush of rage and the rush of guilt—are equally powerful and uncontrollable.

As I wrote earlier, I was diagnosed as bipolar at a late stage. The contrast between the long periods of afternoon sleepiness and my voracious appetite when I was a boy are signs of the possibility that the illness was already in progress. Or perhaps it began to develop psycho-socially only with certain changes that took place in my life. In my adolescent years, my depression was much more common than were manic episodes. The beginning of my obsessive collecting—which in my youth took the form of music albums—was an early sign of bipolar disorder, but by itself would not lead to a diagnosis. As a result, the wild swings that characterize the disorder—between unexpected stretches of sadness that laid me low and moments of excessive, sometimes violent, agitation—were not clear to the doctors I consulted until it was too late. During my first therapy sessions, without medication, or later, in 1989 and 1999, I was treated as a typical depressive, without manic or euphoric swings. The treatments for these two pathologies are very different, and confusing them can have tragic consequences.

I don't lose control with the same frequency as those who suffer from serious bipolar disorder. Some people I know with cases of serious bipolar disorder in the family chuckle when I say I am bipolar. They know how the disease can make someone completely unfit for social and practical life. In my case, the disturbance more frequently appears as a sort of mental agitation, an increase in certain obsessions, and severe insomnia. Until recently, I constantly raised my voice during family arguments. Not today. Bouts of fury—directed against walls, glass objects, people—have become rare. At the slightest sign of them I fall back into self-recrimination, as though I have allowed my bipolar tendencies to spiral out of control. A typical sufferer of bipolar disorder might repeatedly experience this sort of reaction, inflicting enormous suffering on those close to him. Mood-stabilizing medications are crucial at such moments. At any rate, no medication, no matter how effective, is capable of entirely relieving someone with bipolar disorder of all mood swings. It is the magnitude of such fluctuations that, with effective treatment, becomes tolerable or nearly innocuous.

There was a single occasion when I screamed at a colleague at Companhia das Letras, and minutes later I wrote an apology letter to the entire staff, in which I revealed that I am bipolar. I called my UK partners—Penguin had just invested in the publishing house—and let them know: "I lost my patience, and I mistreated an employee. It's my obligation to report it: in fact, you should know, if indeed you don't already, that I am bipolar." They got a kick out of my call, and had a good laugh as they told me that a top executive of Penguin in the US at the time had a similar incident once a day.

I acted similarly in publicly apologizing for attacking a person who insulted me at FLIP, the annual literary festival in Paraty, Brazil. The incident made all the papers. I have yet to get over it. I sometimes think I'll be remembered for that public brawl and not for the books I've published. I attribute these temporary losses of control to my bipolarism, and the sense of shame is deep. This sudden rush of blood to the head is terrifying. The night I lost control in an argument with my mother—with whom I have a very good relationship, but who can get on my nerves—and stepped on the gas pedal and ran the car onto the sidewalk was without a doubt one of the worst moments in my life. It lasted seconds that haunt me to this day.

Shortly after such an event, I am transformed into the world's most penitent man. Or else I cry or sink into utter silence. I turn to Lili, asking what I've done. These fits of rage are the absolute exception in my experience as a bipolar person, but they lay me low and never leave my mind. My manic periods, more frequent in my case than depressive periods, take the form of hyperactivity and anxiety. If I didn't take antidepressants and mood stabilizers, it would be impossible for others to work with me.

On a trip with the Chazit group, I caught a glimpse of just how deeply my father's blow to my cheek had impacted me, and would even decades later. At the campsites we set up, most often on a rural property in Cotia, we would have training sessions in Krav Maga, a fighting method developed by the Israeli Defense Forces, now in vogue as a self-defense tool. Each class began with a new technique and then proceeded to a barbaric ritual in which we were to fight among ourselves as our peers formed a circle around us. The match began with each combatant slapping the other in the face. One time, I was chosen to fight a guy a little shorter but much stronger than I was. He was a tank. After he delivered that first slap, I lost my composure and, instead of responding with a ceremonial slap of my own, I leaped over and took him to the floor with a violent judo blow. On the floor, I choked him until instructors stepped in, stopping me before I could do some real damage. On another occasion,

I pushed a guy down the bleachers when he refused to sit down after the opening whistle for a Santos game at Pacaembu Stadium. Now and then, I pick a fight with overly aggressive security guards or ushers, as I did on a recent family trip to Rome. Many times Lili finds herself warning me, or even holding me back. Picking a fight with the police can only lead to disaster, but I don't always keep this in mind or manage to control myself. The arrogance of customs officers at airports is a huge problem for me. It doesn't take much before I'm spoiling for a fight, spewing insults their way, as though I had some real power to challenge abusive authorities.

Lili is always the one who takes control and prevents me or the entire family from having problems. Not long ago, as I was arriving in New York, a policeman humiliated me. Lili wasn't there, and this time they very nearly had me arrested.

These increasingly rare behaviors may be nothing more than the sign of a typical hothead, but to me they feel more like bipolar loss of control. Over the years, my voice has become softer, my angry words rarer, and perhaps as a result I give the impression that I'm a man at peace, free of major internal conflicts. My tone of voice is deceptive.

Perhaps there are those who do sense something of what's going on within me. Those who have been part of my life for a long time must have noticed, especially those who worked at Companhia das Letras in the beginning. At that time, I was terribly full of energy and conviction. On the other hand, I did everything with a deep irritability, today under control thanks to the right dosage of medication. What's more, my energy level was higher, and my convictions stronger. I knew exactly what I wanted to do as an editor, and I let my obstinate temperament run unchecked, always convinced it was what was best for the publishing house. Even today, I haven't completely rid myself of my excessive determination, though it's nothing compared with the old days.

My near-religious devotion carried over to the books. I treat my authors with a mix of idolatry and a duty to protect.

From the very beginning of my professional life, at Brasiliense, I brought fanaticism to the details involved in the work of publishing books. With this temperament, I made the lives of those I worked with both easier and more difficult.

In the early years of Companhia das Letras, I thought

it was my personal obligation to make all of the company's decisions. After the publishing house grew, I didn't always want to make them, but if a colleague showed any reluctance or hesitation in doing so, I hastened to find solutions. My exaggeratedly assertive behavior sent a different message from the one I intended. In some way, I wanted to stimulate my colleagues' independence, yet at the same time I held them back with my way of behaving. My door was always open and people got used to running ideas by me, because I never turned a question back to them without an immediate response, the key to the solution. I made many decisions as wrongheaded as they were hasty. Today I hope I've learned to delegate better and allow my younger colleagues to succeed or fail on their own.

During periods of elevated agitation and lower medication, I remained capable of reading a manuscript, writing a letter, and answering the phone all at the same time. This compulsion is perhaps even more pathological than angrily punching a hole in the drywall or shoving a person who was blocking my view at the soccer stadium.

NINE

STROSZEK

As a kid, I could often be found at my grandparents' place across from the leafy Praça Buenos Aires. I felt extremely relaxed around Giuseppe and Mici, thanks to the doting of my grandmother, who always had a great time with me until the last minutes of her long life, and to chats with my grandfather, who from my early childhood treated me like an adult in short pants. My parents might not have always known what to do with me; they saddled me with responsibilities inappropriate to my age, but they did so almost without realizing it. Giuseppe, no. For some reason, he decided that his heir would, from a very young age, be someone he talked to eye to eye, as an equal.

Giuseppe would have liked to have more children, but Mici didn't feel the same way. They had worked hard during the war and afterward, and they had arrived in Brazil in a good position. He was your typical Jewish entrepreneur. But he had other attitudes that were hardly common to his generation. He wasn't looking to make a fortune at any cost; he felt at home in Brazil, he became a citizen and enjoyed calling himself a patriot. He valued the fact that he was able to enter the country using his real name—without having to disavow the Jewish religion. He was fond of saying that tax evasion was Brazil's great ill, and he was proud to proclaim that everything sold at his factory, down to a simple greeting card, came accompanied by a receipt. He refused to get rich through tax evasion, a practice typical to many business owners in that era. He looked after the company's more than one hundred employees as if they were his own children, giving them advice, lending them money, and helping them to make personal decisions. He was honest to the bone. At a difficult point in his marriage, Giuseppe told my grandmother that he'd transferred his affections to another person. Nothing had happened between him and the secretary to whom he was referring. But my grandmother reacted very badly, took a few more pills than usual, and ended up in the hospital. I believe it was not in fact a serious suicide attempt but rather an act of desperation, a cry for help.

During my worst depressive crisis, at the age of forty-three, I was in search of the same thing, to an extreme, though my motives were more complex. I considered myself to be in a much worse state than Mici, much more seriously depressed. Today, I am certain that I didn't want to kill myself, that I felt completely lost, most of all on account of medications that weren't the right fit for my bipolar disorder. As for my grandmother's act of "madness," it was of course kept from me, though I could sense something in the air. Fifty years later, when my mother told me what had happened, it was as if I already knew.

I spent many weekends with my grandparents. Sometimes I would ask to sleep at their house during the week, because there was a small television in the room where I slept. When RecordTV began to broadcast so-called music festivals—in reality, competitions—I found a way, during the final rounds, to sleep there, and left the TV on at low volume late into the night. I will never forget the finale of the 1967 festival, whose top four places were split among some of the greatest Brazilian artists of that or any era: Edu Lobo, Gilberto Gil, Chico Buarque, and Caetano Veloso. I must have watched it all at the lowest volume, afraid of being found out. The next day, my excitement over the competition kept me from falling asleep in class.

It's possible my grandparents knew that I was sneaking a peek at the festivals but pretended not to notice. I also tended to find a way to sleep at their house on Thursdays, when the program *Esta noite se improvisa*, where guests had to sing a song that contained a word chosen by the presenter, would show on TV. Chico Buarque and Caetano Veloso were the duo whose songs constantly traded positions atop the show's leaderboard. I couldn't watch these programs at my parents' place, not even in stealth, because the only television was located in the living room. I was given permission every day to watch some afternoon series, such as *Get Smart*, *Hogan's Heroes*, *National Kid*, and *Bat Masterson*. On weekends, I began watching afternoon soccer matches, or else night games when my parents would go to a nightclub called Baiuca with friends. Together with Nilda, the cook who lived with us, I enjoyed some live shows that weren't exactly quality entertainment. We would watch a funny professional wrestling show called *Telecatch*, with Rony Cócegas and Fantomas taking on Ted Boy Marino, or the sensationalist crime and variety shows. On these shows one saw reenactments of crimes that were as gruesome as they were second-rate; mediums performing séances on live TV; and aspiring artists, called "rookies," humiliated before an audience that was out for blood. Nilda and I, or much later Maria, the other maid who worked with us during my childhood, would spend hours watching that garbage, but I think what mattered most to me was that I wasn't alone, and I had the freedom to watch television late into the night.

THE STAY WITH MY GRANDPARENTS that had the greatest impact on me lasted an entire month when my parents took a journey around the world, visiting the United States, Mexico, and several countries in Europe. The trip took place in June, when my birthday falls. My parents sent postcards and letters from each city they visited, but for the special date they managed to send, via courier, an embroidered Mexican sombrero, much too big for my head, which I wore while my grandparents sang "Happy Birthday." Later, they also sent a postcard from Acapulco and photos of the two of them there. On the postcard, a man could be seen leaping from a cliff, and in the photos they looked handsome and happy. Some years later, I would watch two films, one a Tarzan movie shot in Acapulco, in which the hero leaps from the heights, and one with the Mexican comedian Cantinflas, a Tarzan parody that takes place in Mexico. This last one I watched with my grandfather in São Vicente, near the Brazilian port city of Santos. At any rate, the figure cut by Johnny Weissmuller, hero of the jungle, who had been a champion swimmer, must have fused with the image I had of my father. André had a build similar to that of the movie and TV star, and he enjoyed swimming a great deal. In real life, people would say he looked just like Danny Kaye and Kirk Douglas.

As my father grew older, images of that trip would come back to me, and I came to see him as a Tarzan out of his natural habitat. I set out to discover what exactly happened with Johnny Weissmuller, who had never managed to reinvent himself in another role. In the end, he was buried near Acapulco, in a spot that's since fallen into a state of abandon and is now used to graze cattle. It was the Tarzan film in that city that had the greatest impact on his career. It's said that Weissmuller wanted to jump from the towering cliff, a feat managed only by local divers. He was restrained by them and by the production crew.

Many years later, Weissmuller would come to my mind as I watched my father's physical decline. I could see André's death approaching slowly but wasn't sure how to help him. He wasn't just sad but old and tired. At that moment, the suffering that his silence always brought me became unbearable. There were long silences followed by complaints that were impossible to remedy. His sadness wounded me more and more.

During the years I worked with my grandfather, that is, until his death, my father was relegated to the background. Work quarrels spilled over into his personal life and put his marriage at risk. As an old man, he would come to my house one night a week. He would always show up early, and he became irate whenever he didn't find me there. We would also grab lunch once a week. At times, he would openly complain about his marriage and ask for my help, but mostly we didn't have much to talk about and every encounter felt like a challenge. Today I reproach myself for having longed for those encounters to end, for becoming distracted or sighing to myself while my father was talking, or even when he fell into an inconsolable silence.

THE QUARRELING AT CROMOCART drove me from the business that was destined to become mine. It's possible I already knew I would never follow the script of heir, though I had studied business administration, lacking the courage, even at eighteen, to tell my parents and grandparents that I wished to follow my own path in the humanities. Later it became clear that if I was to imitate someone, I wanted to imitate my grandfather and build my own business. In the beginning, I thought I would simply become a university sociology professor, researching the field's application to business administration. At the Fundação Getulio Vargas (FGV), I was diligent in my studies in that area. Much later, I applied myself to the books of Michel Foucault in particular. I wrote a paper about the workings of correctional institutions based on *Discipline and Punish*, the French philosopher's work about prisons, and Erving Goffman's concept of "total institutions," which also included mental institutions. Today, having abandoned a career in sociology, I'd likely feel ashamed of that paper.

At some point, I figured out that every department at FGV was supposed to have an intern. I went to plead my case to the professor who headed up the humanities department. He couldn't say no, but he also had no plans for an intern. He hired me and decided I would go to the library and choose sociology books to read, keeping a list along the way. He did not say what I ought to read. And so I designed my own humanities track, beginning with the classics: Émile Durkheim, Max Weber, Karl Marx, and later the great Brazilian sociologists, like Florestan Fernandes and Fernando Henrique Cardoso, among others. After finishing my reading, I would deliver an updated list to Professor Esdras Borges Costa. One fine day, as I left the room, I looked back just in time to catch him throwing my notes in the trash. In a political science class with Professor Vanya Sant'Anna, I applied myself to such a degree that it was difficult to write with my own words on exams. I remember one exam on the subject of Antonio Gramsci's theories. I was so prepared, having memorized the Italian thinker's book, that I was worried she would think I cheated. It wasn't the case, but I was awarded a grade of only 85. When I protested, the professor responded that she would give only 100 to Marx, 90 to Lenin or Gramsci, so I shouldn't complain.

I was quite a lefty, an anarchist, and averse to political

parties. Influenced by like-minded professors, I was interested in understanding the disciplinary mechanisms in factories and in industrial psychology manuals. I went so far as to begin a master's program in humanities with this purpose, at the Faculty of Philosophy, Languages and Literature, and Human Sciences at the University of São Paulo, and I also thought of having a small bookstore. But that wouldn't have been enough for me, and life found a way of placing me on an entrepreneurial path like that of Giuseppe's.

As for the possibility of joining the family business, my grandfather, no fool, got straight to the point. On a trip to Buenos Aires, he stepped out for a walk with me and said he sensed that I wouldn't remain at Cromocart, so as not to have to share certain responsibilities with my father. My father, a short time later, did something similar. He pulled me aside to tell me he didn't think it was a good idea for me to go work with my grandfather.

Baba and Deda—as I called my grandparents—play an important role in my short story "Acapulco." My time at their house during my parents' trip and the unexpected arrival of the sombrero on my birthday are at the center of the narrative, while the story of Weissmuller develops in tandem. While I was writing my first book of short stories, my grandmother became seriously ill. She was already ninety-four. I rushed to finish the book so that she could read it. It was worth it. Mici kept *Discourse on Some Blades of Grass* at her bedside until she passed. She often said that the best stories were those in which she played a role. I scheduled a launch event at a bookstore near her house, and she promised she would make it. I saw that she had set up her dressing table, as she'd done in my story, to brush her long hair, always worn in an impeccable bun. But she would not manage to make that dream of ours come true. Her death would come a short time later.

MY GRANDPARENTS DESERVE CREDIT for several of the happier chapters in my life. In her final years, my grandmother told me that she was going to leave less money from my inheritance to me, because she intended to spend a good part of it traveling every year, summering in Europe with me, Lili, and the children. We took incredible trips with her. One of the first was a cruise to the Norwegian fjords. The midsize boat was pretty sophisticated for what we were used to, prompting peals of laughter from Baba. She was truly doing her best to torch all her money on travel. For the traditional dinner where the boat captain would sit at our table, she wore a shimmering dress, as though she were going to her debutante ball. More than eighty years old at this point, she called the other ship passengers "those old fogeys." After other boat trips along the Rhine and the Mediterranean, we did a tour of Tuscany, where we rented a Fiat Ulysse, a jumbo white van. We had so much fun that at the simple mention of the name Ulysses—which we called the vehicle as though it were its proper name—the five of us squirmed with laughter. I would drive Ulysses, and Lili would see to the route. In the back seats, great-grandchildren and great-grandmother practically forgot we existed.

One other trip that makes the list of great moments Mici provided for the entire family was the time we went by bus along the lakes of British Columbia. When we arrived at Jasper National Park, we rented Rollerblades and, without regard for time, circled around a good part of the vast resort. At the end, I dragged my children to the lake, where the temperature was nearing freezing. I jumped in first, and after quickly rising to the surface, I held Júlia and Pedro by the arms as they dived in for a few seconds. My grandmother, a supremely elegant woman who wore European clothing and shoes with buckles on the sides, looked on as though she were living out her last will and testament.

Earlier, when I was single, I spent a beautiful week with her in San Francisco. I was finishing college and still intended to become a sociologist. My parents played their last hand and tried to persuade me to do an MBA at Stanford. Mici chose the best hotel and took her grandson for a visit. The hotel was located on top of a hill in the swankiest part of the city. In the end, I didn't even visit the university of my parents' dreams in nearby Palo Alto, instead spending the days at my grandmother's side. We saw Andrés Segovia in recital and went to a rehearsal by the local orchestra. I saw another concert on my own, featuring Herbie Hancock and Chick Corea playing grand pianos opposite each other, but the most incredible moment was one afternoon when we crossed the Golden Gate Bridge toward a tiny cinema in a garage, where a mini festival featuring the films of Werner Herzog was taking place.

The sun was setting as we crossed the bridge, and the scene of grandmother and grandson in that taxi, with the waning sun creeping toward us through the windows, sums up my luminous relationship with Baba. We were on our way to the shoddiest little cinema that I had ever seen. The strange thing is, I wasn't worried whether the itinerary was appropriate to my grandmother's tastes. As in fact it wasn't. The film that day was *Stroszek*, a film that is as beautiful as it is slow and sad. Anguish washes over the viewer from the opening minutes, when the actor and main character, Bruno S., tests—in real life and in the film—the limits of so-called psychological "normalcy." The drama intensifies and, in the final minutes of the movie, Stroszek kills himself in a ski lift. The scene then cuts, as the camera focuses on a chicken frenetically dancing on top of a spinning record behind a windowed cage. A duck, also confined behind glass, pecks away nonstop at a mallet beating a drum, and a rabbit climbs aboard a toy fire truck, wheels spinning. When the credits rolled and the lights came up, it became clear that my grandmother and I were the only ones in the theater.

We drove back across the bridge in silence. Along the way, I could hear my grandmother tut-tutting and mumbling about the strange film I had made us cross the entire city to watch. Making matters worse, it had been no small feat to hail a taxi from the garage to the Fairmont hotel, two places that could not have been more different. We'd spent an hour at the door of the theater, which looked like a motel; the tiny, elegant grandmother and her tall, skinny grandson with the big hair. I was about to hitchhike when a cab rolled up.

It had never occurred to me before that Mici's wild effort to attract attention, taking too many pills, and mine, cutting my arms—which I would do at the lowest points of my depression—would create a deeper tie between my own story and that of my grandmother. During the film, I can't say whether she thought of what she had done, and my own self-harm was still far in the future. When it happened, Mici was spared from being told. I know that she would have understood, but disappointing her to that degree would have been much too much to bear.

As FOR MY GRANDFATHER, I maintain the vivid image of him teaching me to play chess well before my time. I am facing him across a gleaming wood table with ivory chess pieces. There at the table, my feet did not yet reach the floor. I never especially cared for chess; my mind wandered too much for such a sustained challenge. My grandfather had the same problem—he was hyperactive—but what counted at such moments was the fact that we were seated face-to-face, as peers. Our Sunday trips to the factory were preceded by a stroll through the Praça da República. There, he would buy stamps for his purported collection, which he told me he was compiling. Later he would browse the paintings of naif artists who displayed their work on the ground in the middle of the city square. Almost every week he would buy a painting with primitive landscapes and bold colors, reserving the right to use them in Cromocart prints. He would make the artists sign receipts giving him such permission. They did so willingly, as they knew Giuseppe well and vied for his attention. My artistic taste most certainly was not formed on these mornings but rather in art history classes that my mother and her group of society ladies held, once a week, in our apartment. Their professor was Lisetta Levy, an art critic with an Italian accent and just one leg. Some days I would spend the entire class at my mother's side; others, I would sit on the floor and stare at her friends' legs, my gaze fixed on the professor's lone appendage. Meanwhile, she would speak of El Greco,

Antonio Canova, and Cézanne, but my mind was split between these stories and the odd number of legs on view. After each class, I would leaf through the *Great Masters* collection, which my mother would buy at newsstands and send off to have bound.

The divide between these works and the canvases my grandfather would take to Cromocart could not have been greater, but what counted was that before he bought a painting, he would request my opinion. "This one, or that one?" he would ask. And I had to make a choice.

At the factory, which he opened just for us on Sundays, he took care of things he couldn't do during the week. He tried to entertain me, sometimes placing the gold foil machine for holiday cards of the saints to run under my command. At such moments, I felt a sense of duty as I stamped golden halos on the heads of the little saints, miraculous figures in which we, as Jews, could not place our faith.

TEN

MOURNING

André died, nearly fourteen years ago, following an unsuccessful operation to replace an infected heart valve that was discovered much too late. He had almost certainly been sick for a while, and this must explain his weakened state when we would meet. The strong, athletic man's difficulty walking, on top of his depression and sadness, especially acute at the end of his life, were signs of a slow death foretold.

After he retired, my father's Scrooge-ish side became exacerbated. He refused to undergo a dental procedure because it was too expensive. He needed a bridge and also to replace an implant denture with a removable model, which was too much for his vanity. A handsome man like him didn't want to leave a tooth in a glass in the bathroom before going to bed each night. The infection from the tooth moved down to his heart, which the doctor on duty added to his checklist. André was admitted to the Hospital Albert Einstein with septicemia and a burning fever. I was out of the country on vacation. The diagnosis was endocarditis caused by an infected tooth, a case study easily found in any cardiology textbook.

My father remained hospitalized for a month, in an attempt to avoid, via antibiotics, the surgery from which he would not make it out alive.

When I learned what had happened, I hurried back to Brazil and would visit him two or three times a day. There were many nights I slept by his side. I took care of everything as best I could, without ever hearing a single word from André on the subject. He addressed Lili, Júlia, and Pedro with a measure of joy, but he did not spare me from the eternal debt I incurred by failing to resolve his personal problems. He also had no reason, when it was just me and him, to conceal the fact that he knew that his health was going sideways; at his son's side he demonstrated only sadness and apprehension. During his long hospital stay, major Jewish holidays came and went. André was in no shape to go to the CIP synagogue, but there was a small temple at the hospital for this purpose. It was the first time that I sensed indifference in my father when it came to the prayers. In his wheel-chair, he could think only of himself, of death drawing near. It was the first year that his thoughts were not trained on his father. He went to prayers, with our assistance, wearing a suit that, owing to either his condition or the lack of tie, seemed to sag to one side. He refused to go to the synagogue in a simple hospital gown, but his outfit was a far cry from his typically elegant attire on such occasions. Meanwhile, there was another, starker difference: his eyes were dry. Subjected to the drama of a slow death, André had no tears to shed for his father.

After the surgery, he woke a single time, for a matter of seconds, wearing a terrified expression that I will never forget. Even if he had regained consciousness again, he would have suffered from irreversible side effects, and we asked that he not be resuscitated in case of another bout of septicemia. A few days later, his hour arrived.

I never imagined that my grief over his death would occupy so long a period of my life. Fourteen years have passed, and I don't know if or when I stopped grieving.

I began to visit his grave every year on his birthday.

At first I did not realize the importance this ritual would take on for me.

The Jewish cemetery follows the lunar calendar. On religious holidays, the site is closed to visitors. One year, when a holiday fell exactly on May 20, I was not permitted to visit. Furious, I screamed that I had to meet my father, and I nearly lost control with the poor security guard. The doors remained locked.

Jews have a tradition of laying stones on the graves of their loved ones when visiting. I grabbed a few pebbles from the road and tossed them over the cemetery walls, to symbolize that I at least performed that ritual.

When I visit the Butantã Cemetery, I fervently recite the Kaddish and speak with André. I confide my problems to him, and I ask for his help, something I had stopped doing at a very young age. My father would complain, always reminding me of our pact, and say that I had stopped opening up to him.

At times, Lili or my children accompany me to the cemetery. On one visit with Júlia, we saw that someone had already been there and left a stone atop the grave marker. It was early, and we were quite surprised. My father had faithful friends who were still alive then, but all of them were very old. This took place a few years after I had written my first book of short stories, which, with the exception of "Acapulco," I tend to disavow. Many of them grew out of somewhat unusual situations, and portrayed individuals who tended to be quite gauche, isolated, or otherwise ill adjusted. When she saw the stone on the tomb, Júlia smiled and said to me: "Dad, this is just like one of your short stories."

The suggestion stuck with me, but I was too frustrated with writing to take the risk again. Many years later, I gave it a try. I started a novel with André as the central character. I opened the book with a son who finds a stone on his father's tombstone and asks himself whether the man had maintained a secret love affair. The story grew out of events that actually took place, but there were several passages and story lines that were entirely fictional. These were very weak, lacking a certain substantiveness. The protagonist was a loner whose son visited often. His wife had suddenly ditched him. I named the son Rodolfo. The character, ahead of each visit, would prepare tapes of love duets from Puccini operas, always removing the tenor's voice so that his father could sing along with the world's top divas.

This novel lacking in qualities at least served to allow me to immerse myself in André's story. I read book after book about the Nazi takeover of Budapest in 1944, about the work camps that my father was sent to before he and my grandfather were taken to Bergen-Belsen. I researched postwar Italy and the arrival of Hungarian Jews in Brazil. André had often told me about having Portuguese classes with Paulo Rónai in Rio, and I sought to find out a bit more about the life of the great intellectual and translator, who had also spent time at work camps in Hungary. In addition, I studied the life of Puccini, whose own story I inserted into the action.

Reading about the *Tosca* composer who transformed his heroines into founts of inexorable tragedy gave me enormous pleasure. When I'd decided to insert Puccini into the novel, I hadn't the least idea that he suffered from crises typical of individuals with bipolar disorder, swinging between wild mania during creative periods and deep depression after his operas had premiered in cities throughout the world. Puccini's love affairs during tours, the central motivations for his operas, were set against the character partially based on my father, who found himself unable to fall in love and lived alone, locking a fake diary in an unused bedroom alongside belongings from the daughter he had never had.

At the time I wrote it, I had made my peace with opera. I became a Puccini aficionado, as much on account of the sophistication I discovered in his work as for the association with my father. I visited Puccini's house in Torre del Lago, in Tuscany, where he composed many of his operas, and which was also the site of several scenes in my book. At the very least, during the months that I dreamed of that book, Puccini and my father had a great deal in common. It didn't matter that I was the bipolar one in the family; the unfinished novel brought us together. I never completed the sections involving the composer, in which his death due to a heart problem would forge other fictional ties between him and the solitary old man.

André had told me, the night we watched the documentary about the Warsaw Ghetto, that he had been in Cinecittà in 1946, where he had a role as an extra in *Rome, Open City*. The way he said it, I understood he had worked in the studios, but I was mistaken. When writing a story entitled "Father," I had already done some research and seen that Cinecittà was closed at that time.

My dad had in fact been an extra, and not only in the Rossellini film, in exchange for a meager sum, which ensured that he and other refugees could buy some chestnuts, which they split among themselves. They lived in an abandoned, roofless mansion in Óstia di Roma. But the Italian neorealist films were shot beyond the studio, out in the streets, eschewing grandiose sets.

In search of other vestiges of my father's life, at the time I still thought he had worked at Cinecittà, I set out to research the rest of the films that were made in the studios that were Benito Mussolini's hobbyhorse. I then read that, after being overtaken and then abandoned by the Germans, the studios were made into refugee camps, and I understood my error. My father hadn't acted but lived there. Jews and other refugees were housed in cubicles constructed next to sets that had been used to make films exalting Italy's Fascist regime. An editor at Companhia das Letras uncovered an article about the lives of refugees who were settled in Cinecittà. In addition to a description of the size of the canvas cubicles, there were photographs showing the proximity between them and the abandoned sets and costumes. It was in these minuscule makeshift rooms that Jewish families and other war survivors lived while they waited on word that some country had approved their immigration applications.

An extended stretch of my abortive novel took place in Cinecittà. Once again, it was a tale whose principal offense was too many subplots, and a faux erudition, typical of editors. It lacked a cohesive chain of events, and the characters clearly resented their lack of complexity. In my zeal to include all that I'd read in the plot, I forgot that it is the details that create a plausible narrative. One of the subplots portrayed a German cinematographer who had worked with Leni Riefenstahl, was present during the occupation and pillaging of the Rome studios by the Nazis, and—conscious of the extent to which things had begun to unravel for his country—took refuge there when the Nazis abandoned the city.

While I was reading everything about Leni Riefenstahl and writing this section, I learned that a Bolivian author had published a novel whose protagonist had worked with Leni. Already doubting the quality of what I was writing, and without even reading the book in question, I came to my senses, noting once more the lack of originality that plagued my longer works.

As I was writing, I also sought out a friend of my

father's, Magda, who today lives in the Lar dos Velhos senior home and whom I visit often. At the time, she hadn't yet moved to the senior residence and she invited me to her handsome apartment in the São Paulo neighborhood of Higienópolis. She served tea in fine porcelain, showed me pictures of her granddaughters, and shared with me her experiences with André. She had arrived in Italy after surviving Auschwitz. She had been sent with her husband to the Roman neighborhood of Ostia, where they were placed in the same house as my father. Everyone there was awaiting an Israeli immigration visa. Among the many details of life in Ostia and in Cinecittà, Magda recalled how she had watched my father's role as a film extra on the streets of Rome. She told me that, for the production, André had to wear a Nazi uniform. Her voice breaking, she showed me the numbers tattooed on her arm and said, "Luizinho"—to this day she calls me by this nickname—"I may be an Auschwitz survivor, but I have to confess that your father was one handsome guy in that uniform."

It was Magda who told me of the chestnuts they bought after each shoot to be divided among all of the refugees in their house. She made mention of certain behaviors on my father's part that, to my surprise, showed him to have been a true leader among those camped out in that roofless mansion. Magda and André moved from Ostia to Cinecittà at the time they gave up on going to Israel and agreed to immigrate to any other place. When they decided they'd be fine with coming to America—North or South—they were transferred to the studios. From there, they would set out each day on the streets of Rome, where they looked to sell some of the food and clothing that was donated to them, to put away some money and to pay for their future trip. In the end, they took the same ship to Brazil.

On the night my father told me his life story, he said that he had become convinced that he shouldn't go to Israel the day he had a drink with a Hungarian friend. At the same time, André convinced this friend to change his own destination. One of them had set his sights on Israel and instead went to Brazil; and the other had been headed for America and ended up in Israel. My father convinced his friend that Israel was the only place that a Jew could go. This friend brought my father around to the idea that, after the war, it was better to seek out someplace where there was peace. The almost random way in which visas were issued also led people to change plans. It was like a lottery where the thing in play was the fate of the Jewish people.

It's conceivable, given Magda's report, that my father had a different personality at that time. I'm sure he was already scarred by doubt and guilt in relation to the death of Lajos, but with so much tied to the immediate question of survival, there hadn't been time for his sadness to swallow him whole. Magda told me how, on rainy evenings in the mansion, likely a bombing target abandoned by a high-ranking member of the Fascist army, it was impossible to rest. Everyone tried to take shelter in some corner of the house and prayed for the rain to stop. I don't know if my father slept well on the days it didn't rain, but I'd bet not.

ELEVEN

IN THE DEAD OF NIGHT

It was still quite early when the telephone rang. My mother, her voice terribly somber, asked me to come over immediately. At the time, my parents' relationship was awful, but they didn't separate again for two reasons. My father didn't want to; he was afraid of growing old alone, and occasionally would even say he liked my mother. Besides this, they couldn't agree on a price for the apartment where they lived, which would have to be sold and the proceeds split, or else one of them would have to buy the other's share.

Family dinners each Friday, which began with my father's blessing of the wine and my blessing of the bread, were an act of martyrdom for the entire family. My mother tried to control everything, at the same time pretending she wasn't. My father would grumble left and right, about everything. It was common for the two of them to quarrel at dinner, or at least for the atmosphere to grow heavy.

When I made it to the apartment the morning of the phone call, I quickly understood the urgency. For the first time in their lives, André had lost control and become physical, striking Mirta. It wasn't unusual for him to get worked up during their fights, but only with his words. Everything had happened very quickly and there wasn't anything else to do. Filled with remorse, my father had calmed down, and there wasn't any risk of a violent repeat. My mother's telephone call was a cry for immediate help, another manifestation of their fervent desire that their son sort out their unsolvable problems.

André and Mirta expressed the same age-old hopes they had dumped on my shoulders since I was young. I sat with my head in my hands and said nothing. After some time, I walked to the door and told them that what they were asking wasn't fair; no son deserved to be put in such a position. I think that was the first time I managed to say something along the lines of "You just don't do that, much less to your son," and then I left so as not to cry in front of them. Of all my parents' fights, this was the most violent. It was also the first time I made no secret of my feelings at being put in such a position, smack-dab in the middle of their life together—and with all that responsibility.

I wept the whole way home, unable to go to the publishing house. My children were already grown; Júlia was nearly eighteen and Pedro fourteen. Not infrequently, they, too, had dealt with the crises in my parents' relationship, but they got along well with both André and Mirta, who were always terrific grandparents. That day, I made a decision: I needed to find a way to remember my parents the way I had seen them as a child, or at least, how I had tried to see them—as heroes.

I immediately sat down to write in the tiny room with the enormous computer we had at the time. I told myself I had to do that for my children, to show them how my parents had been, how I saw them when I was a child, but today I know this was merely an excuse. During my childhood, I had been exposed to their constant quarreling; from early on I played a role in keeping the couple together. In writing a book, I wanted to remember another story, one that wasn't caught up in separation, in my parents' flaws, and which would above all reestablish a way of seeing them that would never have led to that morning's events. I wanted to remember the couple as though none of it had ever happened. I was in search of parents and a marriage that in truth never existed.

At the time, they were still handsome, just as in old photos, but I wanted to remember them as people who were always strong, and who had lived out heroic moments during the war. There had, in fact, been heroics, especially on the part of two grandparents of mine, my father's father and, in a certain way, my mother's. My mother herself, while fleeing Yugoslavia at the age of three, had to assume a new name in order to cross the border. And she faced some tough times in terms of health after so much traveling, from Yugoslavia and throughout Italy, from north to south. After contracting scarlet fever, she was held in quarantine in Trieste, unable to see her parents for forty days, in addition to other tribulations. She was only four at the time she arrived there.

Giuseppe had been quick on his feet when the Nazis closed in on Zagreb, where the Weiss family lived. He fled to Sarajevo and then to Italy. My mother told me several times how her father, realizing that the Nazis had forced their way into his hat factory to confiscate it from its Jewish owner, escaped out the back door. He must have already had an escape plan, which was how the family left Croatia and Bosnia without ending up in a concentration camp. My grandfather acted quickly, a source of pride for the rest of his life. These two escapes in the former Yugoslavia were not without considerable tension and danger.

In Italy, where the Weiss family received a hearty welcome, they were sent, after a period living with a Christian family, from one internment or concentration camp to another, almost always overnight. This was the agreement Mussolini had made with Hitler. From one hour to the next, every Jew was rounded up and sent from the houses where they were living to camps, which they could not leave. It's said that there were no mass exterminations in these locales, but this myth has since been contested. In the case of my mother and grandparents, there was only sequestration in various camps, without risk of death.

After seven days inside cattle cars on the way to the Ferramonti camp, Mirta began to experience serious health problems. She was saved by a Jewish doctor whom the family had met shortly after arrival, but she would have issues with her vision for the rest of her life. The choice of the name Rodolfo for my brother who lived only three days was an homage to that doctor at the internment camp, also a Yugoslav.

Later, Mirta was separated from her parents, who would leave her with her grandparents for two years while they went to Milan to earn a living. In the big city, my grandfather worked selling parts to clockmakers, and later with currency exchange. Giuseppe would handle the negotiating and Mici was charged with delivering the currency to clients. Near the end of their stay in Italy, he began to work with picture prints, planting the seed of what was to become Cromocart in Brazil. During this time, living with her grandparents, Mirta watched her relatives resort to all kinds of work to survive. She recalls women she knew who turned to sex work, lured by a contingent of soldiers spread along the borders. Their husbands consented, in light of the money, or even handled their wives' work. Living with her grandparents proved no obstacle to my mother seeing up close the complex relationships that war occasions. When the conflict came to an end, and without her knowledge, her parents wanted to immigrate to Israel, much like André.

They did not receive a visa because the country, in the throes of the Arab-Israeli War, did not easily accept couples with children. According to Mirta, the men who arrived there were handed guns and sent directly to the battlefield. For my maternal grandparents, too, Brazil was a matter of chance.

AND SO, on the morning of my parents' fight I began to write a book that set aside any nonheroic aspect of their lives. *My Life as a Goalie* had grown out of my routine as an only child and was anchored in certain childhood events that allowed me to go back in time and recount things I had heard from my mother in the hours we spent together—at the dining room table on Rua Itambé while she sewed skirts, during our trips downtown to deliver her merchandise, or during her lengthy recovery after miscarriages.

An essential part of the text, however, was based on things we heard from my father on the night of the documentary about the Warsaw Ghetto. Lili was already my girlfriend at the time; she was spending that Shabbat with us and was witness to André's emotion as he told his story for the first time.

In the TV room of the apartment on Alameda Ministro Rocha Azevedo, André told us how, after jumping from the train headed for Bergen-Belsen, he ran like crazy and hid in piles of hay on a farm not far from the tracks. The Nazis set out to search for him. They used enormous scythes to poke around the area where he was hiding. My father felt a steel tip scrape against his head and held his breath. After the guards left, he snuck up on the farm's owner, his arms closing in around the man's neck. He pointed to one of his hands, telling the farmer he was carrying a coin and demanding new clothes, which he would pay for with the only thing in his possession.

He made it to Budapest on foot, dressed in the inconspicuous clothing of a farmer. Near the train station, he got caught behind a police checkpoint, where he was saved by a beautiful woman, who, out of the blue, he grabbed and kissed. The wartime atmosphere was favorable to such acts. Besides, André bet on the fact he was a handsome man, limiting the risk that he would be rounded up by Eichmann's patrols without the necessary documents to prove he wasn't Jewish. The soldiers had a laugh at the kissing couple and then, after some time, left.

Living once again in the city, André began distributing fake passports made by one of his sisters. He was jailed and tortured. He had his fingernails pulled out with pliers. In prison he was stripped naked and repeatedly whipped. After each blow, he was forced to stand up straight, facing the wall. If he faltered and let his nose or forehead rub up against the cement, the blows began again. A fellow partisan who worked with him was killed before his eyes with a shot to the head.

A short time before the Allies liberated Budapest, my father was released by the jailer. He might have captivated his enemy with his simple conversation, or his eyes full of kindness. Until the end of his life, he would call others "good people," whether at the sauna at the Clube Hebraica, at the Clube Húngaro, or at the self-service restaurant he liked to visit. Who knows, maybe he addressed his jailer with a similar expression in Hungarian? I always imagined that the good policemen freed him with words similar to those spoken by Lajos: "Run, son, run."

Many years after my father's death, when I was trying to write that novel about him, there was a story in the

Folha de S.Paulo about World War II survivors living in Brazil who were rescued in Hungary, in 1944, by the diplomat Raoul Wallenberg—a kind of Swedish Schindler who dueled with Eichmann in Budapest. In that year, as the Germans were about to lose the war, the Nazi official had one last goal of killing a million Hungarian Jews. Meanwhile, Wallenberg, a millionaire who had actually parachuted into his country's Budapest embassy, handed out safe-conduct and passport documents to Swedish Jews so they could flee the country.

After a certain amount of time, the duel between the two intensified, and the Swede began to indiscriminately hand out passes to Hungarian Jews so that they could escape this last-minute deportation to extermination camps. According to witnesses, when the situation grew more dire still, Wallenberg could be seen walking alongside the lines of Jews who began their long "death marches" to the camps. He sought to free the greatest possible number of people from their fatal destiny. Many Jews died on their feet—of hunger, exhaustion, and cold—before they even made it to the trains that would take them to Auschwitz, Birkenau, Bergen-Belsen . . .

When the story came out in *Folha*, my mother asked

me whether I knew that my father had met Wallenberg. André had mentioned the Swede to her, without getting into details. Caught off guard, I asked her whether she thought he had worked alongside the diplomat. She couldn't be sure, but she thought it was likely. I imagined that André had in fact collaborated with Wallenberg, or, on the contrary, that my father had perhaps conspired against him.

At the beginning of his stint in Budapest, the Swedish diplomat had been confronted by the underground Jewish resistance, composed mostly of young Jews who dared to rebel against the Nazis. The partisans falsified the visas that, in principle, according to an agreement with Eichmann, the Swede distributed only among his countrymen. They printed fake safe-conducts and handed them out across the city. They weren't willing to accept that the struggle for the liberation of the Jews of Budapest pertained only to Wallenberg's compatriots. And so, for a time, the diplomat and the partisans were fighting in different trenches.

It was only with the escalation of the Nazis' bloody crimes that Wallenberg changed his position, moving to save all Jews regardless of their nationality and working hand in glove with the Jewish resistance. My mother's isolated comment set me on a course to read books about the diplomat and to imagine my father as part of that history. With my novel, I picked up where I had left off with *My Life as a Goalie*. I pictured my father falsifying Wallenberg's visas, and a friend of his working with the diplomat, hoisting the Swedish flag in shelters throughout Budapest. According to the initial agreement between Wallenberg and Eichmann, the flags were to protect Swedish Jews from Nazi operations.

On one occasion, while I was looking for accounts by survivors who had lived in Budapest in 1944, I came upon the memoirs of a Hungarian professor living in the United States. In her book, which was self-published, she related how, at a very young age, she was separated from her parents in that fateful year. Ferried from shelter to shelter, she didn't know where her family members were and feared for their future at every moment. She had no idea whether she would see her parents again, and in fact she never did.

One day, a Nazi official entered the apartment where she was sheltered, secretly occupied by Jews—a single room filled with families who barely knew one another.

At that moment, the future professor was certain her time was up. She recounts, with a sense of relief, that the man in Nazi clothing was a Jewish partisan who delivered counterfeit visas or passports to everyone he could find. She was saved by the angel who, I liked to imagine, might well have been my father. (That Shabbat, he had told us how he wore an Arrow Cross uniform to hand out falsified documents.) This kind of uncertainty surrounding André's past has hung over my entire life, to the extent that I found myself becoming emotional as I read the American's book and got goose bumps as though I were reading about my own father. The explanations he gave us that Friday were not the entire story.

In *My Life as a Goalie*, I tell how, when I was a kid, without knowing much at all about my father, I placed him in the role of Bat Masterson, the shining hero of the old Westerns that played on television, or in the skin of certain characters from operas he enjoyed. I also imagined my father as the National Kid, the flying superhero from Japan. Though André was not Asian like the TV vigilante, murky pasts clouded the histories of both: no one knew the true identity of the National Kid, or the story of my father's past.

In my book, I picture my parents as heroes—on television, onstage, or in real life. This was one side of their lives. I was already a bit grown-up to tell only the heroic parts, but that's what happened.

I wrote the book in six months, saying it was only for the family to read, but the truth is I really wanted to see it published. I didn't mention anything to my parents until the book was ready. I sent them each a copy, signed with a fervent dedication. My mother called me immediately, grateful and very moved. My father went quiet for two days. Those hours were torture for me. I thought I might have broken some unspoken agreement with André. I remembered that he had told his story only that Shabbat, and that he had later refused to tell it to the Shoah Foundation, which maintains an enormous archive with the life stories of World War II survivors. I was racked with guilt, and barely managed to leave the house.

When my father finally called, his voice failed him more than ever. Stuttering and barely cognizant of the anxiety he had inflicted, he said that the book was the best thing that had ever happened to him, that it had provoked such powerful emotions that he hadn't been able to call. He asked me to have it translated into English so he could send the book to his two sisters, Klari, who lived in Australia, and Magda, who lived in Israel.

The first time we met after the phone call, André told me a story he had never breathed a word of to anyone. He said that, on his way home to Budapest, and unsure which camp his father had been sent to, he sought the help of a neighbor whose son was a member of the Arrow Cross militia. The young man did indeed try to help my family, and I believe it was he who informed us of my grandfather's whereabouts in Bergen-Belsen, though he was ultimately unsuccessful in freeing Lajos from the camp. With the war at an end, the Nazi sympathizer was imprisoned by the Russians, who had taken Budapest. His family then sought out my father, asking him to testify in favor of their son, who had, after all, tried to help a Jewish family. As he told me this, André's eyes grew damp, and he justified his actions to me as though I had been in Budapest when all this happened. He said that he couldn't lie by omitting the truth. "I had to defend a Nazi, because he had genuinely tried to help us." After testifying, my father was arrested for collaborating with the Nazis, and jailed in the same location where the

Germans had taken him. His oldest sister managed to secure his release, quite literally screaming, telling them about everything my father had endured in that prison.

I FELT A GREAT SENSE of relief at my father's positive reaction, but it was only after a few days had passed that I saw that my purpose in writing that book was much larger. Beyond telling an idealized version of my childhood story and my parents' life, I was also seeking to realize my unattained and unattainable goal: to bring joy to their marriage. I had said that I wanted Júlia and Pedro to see them as I had when I was a kid, but the truth is I never viewed them exactly that way. What's certain is that the book was intended for Mirta and André. They were the ones I sought to convince of the heroism of those stories, or of those half-fictional characters. I also understand now that the task of bringing joy to their married life was impossible. I arrived at this conclusion forty years too late, after spending an entire lifetime consumed by this aim.

One week after the phone call, I met André for lunch. He looked terrible. Without uttering a word, he put a letter in front of me. It came from a lawyer who said he was representing my mother. It mentioned divorce. My father, who perhaps had placed the same hope in my book as I had, compared my effort with the letter and his marital situation. He said explicitly that my book hadn't helped a thing, and once again demanded the impossible. I sympathized with him, and at the same time I understood my mother. Their life together was untenable. Still, I felt short of breath, and for the first time I intuited what I had been looking to do with *My Life as a Goalie*. The mission of helping or saving my parents was always nuts, but I had not entirely freed myself of it.

In fact, I would fully understand the magnitude of my aim in writing the book only years later, thanks to the help of psychoanalysis. The letter that André received was the most concrete sign that my infantile illusion, cultivated over many years, made no sense. And, strange as it may seem, I hadn't realized it until that moment. I have no one but myself to blame. We don't assume these roles on purpose. No doubt, my personality has always had a pretentious side, since I was a child, that led me to believe I was capable of achieving such unreasonable feats. No matter how much my father demanded more help of this sort, or my mother expressed an outsize dependence on me, it was in my own head that everything fell into place.

At the time of publication of the book, having found great professional success, I harbored some seriously strong convictions, which inundated my work and family life. For other reasons, these same convictions had revealed certain flaws. No one could manage to maintain their psychological health with such confidence. Besides, I did have a measure of self-criticism, and my home life was full of people with considerable personality.

I was constantly judging myself, and shortly before writing the book, or as I was writing it, I began to question my arrogance. Lili had been trying for some time to help me understand how I was acting, and Júlia, now grown, also started to confront me. Her temperament was quite similar to mine, and in her teenage years, on the rare occasion when we butted heads we both went for the jugular. Daughter was unafraid to take on father. At the time I would get flustered and try to turn the tables to put an end to the argument. Later I saw that in many cases she was right. Thanks to the clash of generations, I came to better understand myself.

On the other end of the spectrum was Pedro, who was overcoming early learning difficulties; he had an attention-deficit disorder that hadn't been detected by his school. Had he had sufficient professional help and received the correct diagnosis, he could have been spared considerable suffering. Before this happened, the insecurities he overcame humbled me. Pedro struggled to find his place within the conventional school approach to learning and had revealed himself to be stronger than I was, despite all the problems that he should never have been made to face.

At any rate, it was no easy task to leave my arrogance behind. The process, closely tied to the illusions that I had placed in my first book, brought dark clouds to my life, and a severe depression began to take form.

In our marriage, Lili and I experienced a certain growing apart. This was one of those difficult but normal periods that occur in the most durable and successful unions. Our relationship wasn't in question, but my psychological state didn't help me understand things as such. I wasn't always there when it came to Lili's academic success. Laid low for other reasons, I had difficulty accepting that there was an entire area of her life in which I played no part. Little by little, I grew increasingly fragile and began requiring her total and exclusive attention. The timing couldn't have been worse. Lili had been invited to a conference in Portugal. She asked me time after time if I preferred she didn't travel, and, in my pride and my silence, I insisted that she go. I should have simply humbly asked her to stay. It would have caused her some disappointment, but it would have been the right thing to do.

I quickly became much worse, and Lili had to cut her trip short. Even in a rather unbalanced state, I'm fairly certain I never said what it was I wanted, but she noticed and rushed home. I went to meet her at the airport, flowers in hand and an awful look on my face. I was grateful and filled with shame at the same time. A few days later, we went to our property in the countryside, where we had built only temporary shelter while the house was still under construction. I had insisted we begin work. Lili was absorbed by a new research study and had wanted us to wait for a calmer moment in her professional life. But I had to build that house to fill the void that, little by little, was gaining control over my mind.

I remember that we sat on the upper part of what would come to be the log house, which at the time was only stakes and beams on the steep lot, a house without walls, to be inhabited by the imagination. It didn't matter how much I had been involved in the blueprint and all the research and conceptualization. I was down and out and I couldn't at all envision something approximating the refuge that would become the most important of my life. It would be there, on the border between the states of São Paulo and Minas Gerais, that I would begin my frequent surrender to the gelid rivers, whose sources are to be found a short distance above our property. In the condition I was in, all I could glimpse when I scanned the surroundings of our future house was ruins. My depression tightened its grip.

A short time before this, I had sought out a psychiatrist for the first time. I was experiencing obsessive thoughts and total personal insecurity. She prescribed a strong antidepressant and recommended that we speak daily. That diagnosis contained a serious error. I was medicated as though I had simple depression and not a condition on the bipolar spectrum. During the course of treatment, I would not improve; on the contrary, my symptoms only worsened. I recall that a bit later I was also prescribed an antipsychotic, and that did me tremendous harm. That drug was one of the worst things that ever happened to me. It wasn't that I was out of my mind. I had repeated and incessant thoughts, blew things out of proportion, and saw everything in a negative light. There was no justification for the use of that powerful antipsychotic. I began to lose control. Everything fell apart and changed in a matter of minutes. I no longer had any convictions, much less self-confidence.

One Saturday night, we went to the movies and made an unfortunate choice of film. Long before the end of *Fight Club*, I began to feel bad and left. Lili watched a bit more while I waited outside. My head felt like a garbage disposal. The violence on-screen had taken over and it was as if each punch had landed square on my chin. Sitting in the movie theater lobby, I made an effort not to scream. I ought to have returned to the auditorium and explained the situation to Lili, but I sat still, thinking that she was the one who needed to guess what was going on inside my head. I was in the midst of an intense manic crisis and unable to separate what was happening to me from the outside world, as though I were at the center of everything.

The next day, there was to be a Companhia das Letras event involving several authors. A conversation with children about *My Life as a Goalie* was part of the program. I woke up feeling awful, but stuck to the plan. I thought that the event would do me some good; however, as I spoke about my childhood, the tears started to stream and I almost couldn't make it to the end. That afternoon, at home, my condition grew much worse. I tortured Lili with nonstop chatter, my mind hurtling toward the abyss. She did everything she could, wrote me a tender letter, but I didn't want to hear it. By that time, I was already long gone. I had totally lost control. I walked to the bathroom, locked the door, destroyed the shower door, and cut myself. They were only surface wounds. It was a cry for help and not an attempt to end my life. My confusion and my sadness were absolute.

Lili reached out to my psychiatrist, who asked her to bring me to a recovery clinic. Four of us—including Júlia and a friend of Lili's—went to a remote locale, where the doctor also met us later. I'm fairly sure that, beyond cutting myself, I had taken five or six sedatives, and my head was spinning, not only on account of the pills but from the state of shock that had steadily grown ever since the screening of *Fight Club* and had exploded at that moment.

The antidepressant had made my condition considerably worse. It was intended to raise my spirits, as though I were always down in the dumps, deeply depressed. And so my obsessions became even more unbearable, ultimately causing a serious manic peak.

The clinic where I was taken was legitimate, but I remember very little of it. I know only that I spent a few hours in a tiny room under supervision. Lili went to pick up Pedro at a friend's house and called my parents. It was difficult to see them and experience that role reversal. With time, the sedatives wore off and I realized what had happened. I was slowly overcome by total shame. At first, I don't recall apologizing for the loss of control that overtook me. As my recovery wore on, it was touch-and-go, and whenever I came to my senses, I would apologize nonstop and begin to cry.

It was especially difficult to see my father walk into the tiny room that first day. My mother had always been the stronger of the two, no matter how much she had stuck me in the middle of her own life. She had lost one child after the next and crucially could always count on the support of a very involved father, with whom she had an excellent relationship. By that time, Giuseppe was no longer alive, but his influence remains important to my mother to this day.

André and Mirta were naturally very worried and frightened, but they sought to keep it together. I remember my father's lost expression most clearly, his gaze doing the talking where words failed him. Mirta was more composed, or at least put on that she was. A few hours later, Lili returned and I was released, though under the full-time supervision of a nurse. That night, the nurse slept on a chair in my bedroom. As I remember it, I was forced to endure his company for a month or longer. But it seems that it was in fact a matter of days or a week.

What's certain is that I spent a long period without leaving the bedroom or working. When I had trouble sleeping, or in moments of despair, I would violently beat my feet against the bed, just like my father.

TWELVE

SIDE EFFECTS

At home, treatment continued, but without much progress. At least things were under control, a far cry from my wild mood swings, in no small part thanks to the high dosage of the anxiety medication I had been taking. I believe it was my psychiatrist following these events who began to treat me for bipolar disorder. I'm not certain if she was the one who urged the switch or if it was the new doctor to whom I appealed two months after my meltdown. The fact is that I remember being completely hostage to my medicine. This latter psychiatrist, who had treated a friend of mine, totally changed up my medication. He suffered from too much fame and not an ounce of charisma, or sensitivity. He would come up with catastrophic metaphors, comparing depression to a clothes hanger, capable of accommodating any dark thought. I don't know if it amounted to too much literary rigor on my part, but his simplistic figures of speech were no help. For me, depression was much more than a hanger where bad thoughts hung.

The expectations of a depressed person are renewed with each appointment, or with each change in doctor, but beyond such moments, treatment for a serious depressive crisis is incredibly slow and painful. The patient feels adrift, and not only when he or she resorts to extreme behaviors or in the most serious periods, when things feel out of control. The turbulence is so intense that life appears to be perpetually hanging on by a thread. Medication has its effects on the body, and the constant changes render any hopes for a quick recovery entirely futile. And so, at the beginning of treatment, the ditch only gets deeper.

The misery is such that it's not the patient alone who clings to what the doctors tell him: the family feels they are living the tired metaphor of trying to find the light at the end of a tunnel, when in reality there isn't any. Everyone's life changes. Suddenly the sick person requires their full attention, snatches away any space for individuality, and transforms the family into a single bloc ruled by illness. There is a sort of depressive totalitarianism. The dedication Lili, Júlia, and Pedro showed was moving. They gave me everything they could. We would cry together some days, but most of the time, they stayed strong despite seeing me in my inconsolable state. In the same way that it was painful for me to grow up with parents who needed my help, it wasn't easy for my children to face the abrupt change in their father from practically self-sufficient to a broken man. In this intense period my attacks of guilt mingled with depressive thoughts, spurring prolonged weeping episodes in a vicious cycle that demanded endless patience on the part of my wife and children.

After the explosion, as the depressed person spends his entire time at home, his mind oscillates wildly between an uncontrollable urge to demand total attention, judging every action by family as evidence of love or neglect, and moments of self-deprecation and absolute shame, which provoke endless self-justifications. Because of the wild mood swings caused by bipolarism, I would start crying out of nowhere, in one cycle after another. When it was over, I couldn't even remember why I had started crying in the first place.

I could see the effect my illness was having on Lili

and my children; I could tell they needed to run from the drama or forget it, at least every now and then. But I sometimes misinterpreted this need for air. Lili suffered the most from this. I couldn't stand it when she went to meet a friend for coffee, or when she would spend time at our front door talking to a student who sought advice.

These first months were cruel, and my anxiety only grew worse. We weren't talking about a hanger but an offensive. Treating depression requires considerable time, but the patient is in a hurry. With each disappointment or setback, our internal clock seems to speed up, and it feels like we can't possibly wait. After I improved, I understood that my children and Lili needed to lead their own lives. It wasn't enough to help me; they needed moments to forget about their father's and husband's illness.

A short time before my crisis, I had sought out a former therapist, with whom I'd undergone Freudian psychoanalysis for three years in the 1980s. In those early sessions with Maria Elena Salles—which began when I was working at Brasiliense publishing house—Companhia das Letras had begun to take form. There on the divan, thanks to psychoanalysis, I understood that I needed to create and run my own publishing house. After the company was founded and enjoyed premature success, I began to skip sessions. I couldn't make it to three sessions a week the way deep psychoanalytic work requires. I would invariably miss one of them. It was true, I had many more commitments than I had expected, but I was also drunk on the initial impact of Companhia das Letras. Against my better judgment, I bailed. Sometime later, I ran into Maria Elena on a short flight and she asked whether I thought of returning. Politely but firmly, I told her no.

When my depressive crisis began, I sought her out and she thought it was a better idea that I try to resume treatment with another doctor. We had formed something of a friendship after that flight. She gave me three names; I met with them all but didn't like any of them. The work I had done with Maria Elena made it difficult for other therapists to compete. After my breakdown, I went back to her and we resumed treatment. Initially, Lili had to drive me and wait for each of four weekly sessions. After some time, I went on my own.

Psychoanalysis was one of the most important experiences of my life, and this second round lasted a little more than ten years. Even with the right medication—which was only reached more than a year after my total loss of control—I wouldn't have been able to fully emerge from the crisis without psychoanalysis. What remains of my disorder, and the thing that rears its head now and again, or makes it so that I can't stop taking medication, is basically chemical. I don't know what would have happened if I hadn't gone through this journey of self-discovery, when I often found myself at the edge of the abyss yet managed now and then—thanks to the tools I discovered within myself—to glimpse redemption. That's how we feel after engaging in serious psychoanalysis following a process of self-destruction. Without analysis, I would not have had the tools to grapple with the chemical effects of my depression.

In terms of the medical treatment, the worst was the constant change in medication, the setbacks, the loss of control over mind and body in the midst of the side effects of such an intense chemical onslaught. During rare moments of good humor, I would say that I would make the most of my experience and write a novel entitled *Side Effects*. And in fact, I experienced all sorts of side effects: headaches, drowsiness or terrible sleeplessness, nonstop sweating, tremors in my hands and legs, and consequences in my sex life. By some miracle, I didn't entirely lose my libido; on the contrary, I came to rely a bit on this area of my life, in an attempt to find some pleasure or affirmation of my ego. The medication, meanwhile, made it extremely difficult for my body to function normally. It's a wicked irony, produced by pharmaceuticals that are supposed to save one from depression. In my case, the libido was still there, but with the bulk of the antidepressants I took, it was impossible to find any pleasure. Worse yet, thanks to a mood stabilizer, I had experienced another type of anorgasmia: I began to ejaculate without any pleasure, without feeling anything at all. In fact, I didn't even realize I was ejaculating; it was even less noticeable than peeing. This was one of the most traumatic parts of this period. I was incapable even of physical pleasure, as though my body could give me nothing but absolute sadness.

Sports and sun are essential therapeutic tools, but in the early days you don't feel like leaving the house at all, much less to exercise. I stayed inside, many times in bed, my feet pounding against the mattress. My only relief came from my family's care and the company of our dogs.

Before this deep personal crisis began, I had experienced a medical problem resulting from a surgery for a hernia in the groin, which no doubt contributed to my psychological state. Depression magnifies the tiniest pain, and constant pain only deepens depression. During the operation, the surgeon overtightened the belt that is placed in the abdomen, which led to a constant pain in my testicles that would last two or three months.

I saw several urologists who closed ranks with their professional colleague and told me that I had an inflammation in the region near my testicles, more specifically epididymitis. They never blamed their colleague for his basic error during the operation.

The offices of Dr. Drauzio Varella, a renowned physician and writer, were near the publishing house, and, after learning of my pain, he would come to see me, locking the door to my office and injecting me with anti-inflammatory drugs, which helped some but only temporarily. The mysterious pain was diagnosed properly only when Drauzio took me to see Dr. Dario Birolini—the master of all surgeons in São Paulo. Dr. Dario explained that the blood wasn't circulating properly in the region where I was operated on, though with time this would be corrected. He told me that the surgeon, a former student, had "done his homework too well," tightening the belt more than he should have. What's certain is that the constant pain in a sensitive location laid me low just before my worst period of depression. This was a serious contributor to my destabilization.

A bit later, cured of my surgeon's excessive diligence with his homework but very depressed, I wanted to resume a normal life and take advantage of the moments when I still had some energy. Nonetheless, the antidepressants and mood stabilizers got in the way.

Little by little I began to leave my bedroom and walk through the house. My psychiatrist said I would be fine on my own, seeing how Lili needed to go to work. I had to come to the understanding that Lili had to go on living her life; she couldn't always be at my side. I would sit for long hours in the garden or the laundry area. Bartolomeu, one of our dogs and also one of the most important parts of my life, would lick my face as I sat inconsolably in his company.

Later on, the mood stabilizers prescribed by my new doctor—medications that, for bipolar patients, balance out the antidepressants—induced serious fog and an encroaching depersonalization. I couldn't feel anything, I couldn't recognize myself—on account of the turbulence brought on by depression, yes, but also the total loss of self brought on by the medication. My manic crises became ever rarer; on the other hand, I felt like a vegetable. My endless weeping eased, my volatility tapered. In return, there was nowhere for the sadness to escape.

Everyone's reaction to medication is different. What works for some is a death knell for others. I couldn't handle Depakote or Depakene for long periods. They brought on the same fog. We tried other stabilizers. Though with time I overcame the initial impact, for many years I felt that the antidepressants got in the way of certain feelings— or more precisely, the release of these feelings. I'm quick to tear up in moments of sorrow or when overcome by emotion, but with these medications, years passed when it was impossible to cry. I felt the urge, but my body, under strict orders from my daily chemical intake, would not allow it. One of the most difficult moments was two years ago when Margot, one of our dogs, died. Lili and I were in New York. I tried to rush back but was too late. The pain inside was immense, but the tears never flowed. It's much easier to overcome our sadness when we can feel it stream down our faces, tighten at the back of our throats, knock the air out of us.

TWO DAYS AFTER the dark Sunday when I cut myself, I began to write a book, in longhand, mania at a high. It was a novel about a pianist who decides to give up his career after attending Dinu Lipatti's last concert, in Besançon. The great Romanian pianist, plagued by late-stage cancer, did his best to make it through this final concert. But he was unable to finish the program: in the end, Chopin's Waltz op. 34, no. 1, scheduled to close the program, was left untouched. Lipatti is a real person, and I believe the concert in Besançon took place more or less along these lines. In my imagination, Lipatti's wife stood backstage, trying to gauge whether he would make it to the end or not. The pianist at the center of my story romanticizes music as an art form beyond the limitations of the human body and mind. Seeing his idol falter, he surrenders to the fragility of human existence and abandons his career. He recounts his life to a boy who is going to school without his father for the first time, who gets off at the wrong bus stop and misses the opening bell.

The boy is caught waiting at the curb for the end of the school day and thinking of an excuse to give his father. He has failed in his first act as an independent person. He comes upon the long-legged pianist, who kindly asks if he may sit next to the boy on the curb.

This almost-novel was terrible, and in this case I didn't even need to show it to an editor to know that. All I needed was for my depression to lift somewhat as my treatment progressed, and to see Lili's reaction upon reading it. The scene where the boy gets off at the wrong bus stop ended up in a story of mine many years later. An entire book that was reduced to a few lines in another story. I remember that I began writing it at the time I was still being looked after by a nurse. Even his breathing down my neck couldn't curb my furious need to write. In those days, my mania was most certainly not under control.

On her second visit to Brazil, Susan Sontag, an obsessive music lover like me, asked me during lunch whether I had ever heard the live album from Dinu Lipatti's final recital. I smiled and said, "Yes, I know it, and you have no idea how close this album is to me." It had been only two and a half years since the beginning of my crisis, but of course I didn't so much as mention the book that I had already abandoned.

It's a curious thing the way these frustrated novels that are so much a part of my life occupy my memory. The fact that I wrote about a pianist disillusioned with art and about a boy who falters during his first act of independence is more useful as a key to my psychological state, or my life up to that point, than as good writing. It would seem that all of those books, long since condemned to the trash bin, were written to feature here, in this book of memoirs. They serve to define me by what I did not publish. And they allow me to make light of those poor characters whom I once thought to create.

THIRTEEN

THE EDITOR AS FICTIONAL CHARACTER

Before the almost-novel written by hand, I had already attempted to write another, at the time I had my first depressive episode. This happened around nine years before the deep crisis of 1999.

At the 1989 Frankfurt Book Fair, Companhia das Letras had a terrific year, which helped earn the publishing house an international reputation. The credit for this goes to Ana Miranda's novel *Bay of All Saints and Every Conceivable Sin*. Following the book's critical and popular success in Brazil, I prepared to sell international publication rights, at a time when almost no works of Brazilian literature made it beyond the country's borders. My strategy worked out better than I expected. Such was the hubbub that the best publishing houses around the world were compelled to make blind offers—that is, without reading the book. A spontaneous bidding process began, and a good part of the global editorial market set its sights on our book. A battalion of editors who had heard about the novel in the book fair halls sought me out at the group stand for Brazilian publishing houses, a locale notable for the fact that the ferns outnumbered the books. I spent no time at the fern farm. Seeing as I hadn't expected anyone to come to me, I had scheduled meetings at other stands, to purchase rights for novels and essays from various countries. Unable to find me, publishers left their offers—based, at most, on readers' reports from some German publishers who had received the book prior to the fair and had time to read it.

That's how Frankfurt works: a book's reputation snowballs across the convention center halls. One editor mentions something to another, who then relays the information to a third, and so on and so forth. The fair works like a spiral of illusions, which the best publishing houses climb aboard, without reading.

I decided to reject the offers, responding that I would

instead give everyone a chance to solicit their own readers' reports from someone who could read Portuguese, so they would know what they were buying.

The fair at an end, I went with Lili for four days to Venice and Milan. In Venice, we decided on a modest hotel that had purchased its first fax machine the same week we arrived. Messages streamed from the contraption until they inundated the tiny lobby. Few editors had found the time to get a reader's report, but all the same they sent their offers via fax to the Companhia das Letras offices. From there, they were sent to the hotel. It was fun to come back from strolls along the canals and through palaces and read the mountain of paper filling up the printer spooler. I continued to reject the blind offers, reiterating that everyone would have two weeks to read the book.

An unexpected development caused us to make an early return to Brazil. My grandfather, suffering from a lung ailment, had taken a turn for the worse and his days were numbered. While we were still traveling, he followed our Italian junket with map in hand. A few days after our return, Giuseppe died. Up to that point, I had lost only my paternal grandmother, who lived just a short time in Brazil, when I was too small to remember her; my maternal great-grandfather, whom I remember only in photographs; and my maternal great-grandmother, whom I would visit often but whose dementia plagued her for years. I would visit her on Sundays at a nursing home in the São Paulo neighborhood of Vila Mariana, the same place where my father's two friends lived. Toward the end, she no longer recognized anyone and passed the time singing Sephardic songs in Ladino. Her voice had that piercing dissonance of the ancients. It was a beautiful thing to listen to her faltering singing, its constant refrain in a language that was familiar yet incomprehensible. Her eyesight was terrible and she had trouble making sense of what she could still hear, and so those songs that no one understood were her only form of communication with the world, and with herself.

My grandfather's death was the first to leave a serious void inside me. Despite his snubbing of my father at work, Giuseppe was a fairly cordial man. He diplomatically avoided confrontation, figuring out how to do things the way he wanted without quarreling. We adored each other. I made use of the fact that the family's many conflicts were never brought out into the open and I got along with everyone. I sought to fulfill everyone's expectations.

My grandfather showed me respect, and I made a sincere effort to return his premature trust. When he passed, I understood the meaning of death. When I decided to leave Milan to make it back in time, I panicked, fearing I wouldn't get there while he was still alive. I had an agreement with my mother that she would warn me if his condition worsened. Mirta, at Giuseppe's request, phoned me only when it had become clear that he would not overcome the swelling in his lung. The trick was calling me without telling my grandfather, who always had the map of Italy at hand. I managed to see him while he was still lucid, but only for a few short hours.

When I had founded Companhia das Letras, Giuseppe and André were my partners and gave me two rooms in the back of the printing business to use for the publishing house. Deda would come see me every day, and if I was with an author, he would say: "This one used to be my grandson. Now, I'm Luiz's grandfather."

During the Kaddish, the prayer that Jewish people recite in the home during the week following the death of a family member, always at dusk, I started to receive phone calls at my grandmother's house from editors who had managed to track me down, hoping to discuss their offers for *Bay of Saints and Every Conceivable Sin.*

With each refusal, the blind offers went higher and higher, doubling or tripling. Carol Brown Janeway, a friend of mine from Knopf who steered clear of this mad dash, would howl that I had planned it all out that way— to her mind, my refusals were a marketing strategy in search of larger advances, but I would never have done this on purpose. In fact, the international episode around *Bay of Saints* proved an excellent chance for a number of editors to become familiar with the Companhia das Letras catalog. Many attested to the quality of the titles published in those early years and began to invite me to private dinners or exclusive cocktail hours.

Bay of Saints, despite being a very good book, didn't bring a profit to international publishers, so high had the advances gotten by the end of that unexpected bidding war. As a result, I began to ask myself questions about the way the market worked, about the methods—not always especially deep or literary—of the top publishing houses around the world, which I came to know more closely. Some months after the fair, I suffered a serious tear in the ligaments of my ankle. I had to undergo an operation that required two months of rest and physiotherapy. During that time, I felt myself lose enthusiasm and watched as my idealistic view of the work of a publisher waned. Some of my professional convictions were demolished. I stopped going to nonessential book fairs, including one in the United States that was still very popular at the time. It was my first glimpse of adult depression.

In response to my growing disillusionment, I began to dream up a novel, but I produced only a few pages. The story centered around an editor with a romantic view of literature, the same way the pianist I would write about years later had a mythical view of music. The editor in my book became disillusioned with the profession's commercialism, lost his mind, and began selling rights for a nonexistent novel in Frankfurt. He ginned up a cover, jacket copy, reviews, and bestseller lists—all fake.

The subject of the imaginary novel was the unearthing of a score Berlioz had composed based on an obscure Shakespeare play. The book was sold to publishing houses around the world, and the editor returned to Brazil with an obligation to write it. He took refuge in the town of

Atibaia, and from there sent a letter to his girlfriend. It was a ridiculous parody of Brazilian president Getúlio Vargas's final letter before taking his own life in 1954. The missive was also a jumble of references to the editor's favorite writers—from Raymond Chandler to Jorge Luis Borges, Machado de Assis to Albert Camus. I believe it ended with "I leave history to enter Literature." The girlfriend then deduces that the editor has departed for the city where one of the cited writers lived and sets off in search of her partner, following a trail based on the most important works of each quoted writer; all the while, he is actually to be found in a place without the least literary appeal. In the end, in Atibaia, he manages only to write a story, a very good one but not enough to deliver to the editors who had bought the rights to a novel.

I told Rubem Fonseca, the most famous Brazilian short story writer of the time, about the book. I was so out of my mind that I asked whether he would write this story—of excellent literary quality, to be sure—to be inserted into the middling novel I was writing. Rubem responded sagely: "The excellent story is the easy part. The tough part is writing the rest."

I don't know which of the novel drafts that I wrote

during my depressive stretches was worse. Both reveal a total lack of talent for long-form fictional narrative and an outsize belief in preconceived ideas, without deep exploration of the characters. The same would come to pass later with the novel about my father, though the first two, written under varying degrees of manic agitation, were of even lower quality. Those two near-novels were not in fact much better metaphors than the one used by the famous psychiatrist. They were more freewheeling. At least I had the excuse of the mental state in which I wrote them.

Years working in publishing ought to have helped me to avoid embarking on such ill-fated ventures. As it turned out, I always had fewer illusions as a writer than critical sensibilities as a reader. Or I received the help of others. Both books came to be at moments when my self-criticism was impaired by the frenetic pace of my inner life.

Whatever the case, the novel about the editor reveals a time when certain misgivings about the profession threatened to overwhelm me. Still, there's a great deal of pretentiousness, disguised as parody. My drunkenness with this second period of professional success, from Brasiliense to Companhia das Letras, showed signs of abating. The figure of the idealistic editor now appears to me like a rough draft of the would-be pianist. And my mini depression in 1990 was a dress rehearsal for what was to come, much more intensely, nine years later. I also came to question other convictions with time, in a process that might have spared me a more serious ego trip but at the same time pushed me into depression.

The treatment for my first symptoms of depression in 1990 was administered by my general practitioner. I took Prozac, but I had an allergy that caused swelling in all of my joints and red splotches on my skin. The doctor was ecstatic with the "amazing" case on his hands, which for him was an interesting clinical event. His characterization and the allergy that spread across my body led me to ditch both the GP and the Prozac.

Whatever the details, during this prelude or seed of depression, the editor and musician who mythologized art and became disillusioned were one and the same with the boy who would have liked not to grow up so fast.

FOURTEEN

MEMOIRS

I spent the first three months after my severe depressive crisis of 1999 entirely shut off from the world. After this period, I began to improve and returned to work. My return to the publishing house was an emotional one. Only two people knew in any detail what had happened to me; others likely heard that I suffered from depression. I had an outpouring of support that day, I wept like crazy, and it felt good.

But life still wasn't back to normal. At the end of the previous year, we had celebrated the completion of the main house on our property in the country, the one that had still been under construction when Lili returned from Portugal. We invited two couples, some of our closest friends, and their children. These friends were the only people who had been there throughout my crisis. It was the official launch of the house of our dreams.

It seemed everything would work out at the beginning of that year, but on New Year's Eve, one of our dogs became startled by the fireworks and went missing. We spent two desperate days looking for Fred, who had taken shelter in the basement-like area of the tiny house we had built near the river to supervise construction. After this, the weather took a definitive turn and the house was surrounded by clouds for days. We couldn't see anything farther than arm's length away. The situation would have unnerved anyone, but it was especially untenable for someone with depression. Nature works as metaphor in the mind of a depressed person, who needs to see clearly and to bask in the heat of the sun. At that point, it was only me and Lili with our children and our friends' children. We knew that the bad weather was a risk for someone with depression, but at the time I thought I was almost completely recovered, and I just shrugged at the forecast. The long storm of 1999–2000 on the Serra da Mantiqueira was without precedent, then or after.

In the mountains, I realized I was far from better as

the thick clouds bore down on me. To make matters worse, with each passing day we received the news that more mudslides had closed the road in various spots. The power went out, and after days without electricity, the frozen food went bad. The encroaching clouds and the road conditions caused us to panic and we decided to go home. We left in a hurry and by some miracle avoided obstacles on the way. Given my state, encountering any would have been a disaster. The property caretaker's family left, too, and found themselves stranded for an entire day on the road to Campos do Jordão. The caretaker had only made it out of his house with the help of a vine.

After that frustrating year-end, Lili wanted to take me to the seaside. We hadn't received authorization from the psychiatrist for her to go anywhere with me alone. The presence of someone to help in an emergency was mandatory, so my mother-in-law came with us. Shortly after we arrived, torrential rain descended on the north coast of São Paulo state. At the same time, a problem with the boiler caused flooding—all this on our first night.

Like storms, floods of all kinds can intensify a depressive crisis. To make matters worse, as she tried to get the house dry, Lili fell and broke two ribs. I was barely any use at all, incapable of so much as grabbing a squeegee, and I had trouble helping Lili to the hospital. The incident left me terrified, almost paralyzed. Looking out for others had always been my forte, but when we're depressed we lose even the most fundamental parts of ourselves.

With the heating broken, we moved to another house, Lili doing her best to disguise her pain. We walked along the beach—when she could manage. These strolls did some good, but my medication was still not right, and a full recovery remained a distant reality. After that stay, I was in no rush to return to the beach.

Other trips we took at the time likewise didn't end so well. After I'd improved some, I told Lili I wanted to take her to New York. Once there, I had a serious episode, despite the fact that we went to the theater or a concert every night. In the middle of *The Lion King*, then the top show on Broadway, the tears began to stream. Not because the heart of the plot is the loss of a father, but out of pure loss of control or extreme self-pity. The sight of a grown man choking back tears during *The Lion King* made for a ridiculous sideshow. We were going to Broadway to please Lili, who has been wild about Disney movies ever since she was a little girl. The outing was intended to prove that I didn't always need to be the center of attention and was capable of doing something for no other reason but to please her. It didn't work out.

On another occasion, thinking I was in good shape, I went with Pedro to Bonito, an ecotourism destination in Brazil. There I discovered that depression can ruin even a beautiful view. What caused me the greatest anguish was the excessive tranquility of the plains there in Mato Grosso do Sul, the lack of any variation in the landscape. The beauty of the perpetually clear skies and the crystalline rivers became lodged in my throat. It was like the empty skies were nothing more than an echo of my emptiness inside. I tried everything to hide my state of mind from Pedro, soldiering on through the end of our trip.

It's only natural to think that after so much time, and being healthy now, I could look back on events in Juquehy Beach and New York with typical Jewish humor, finding the tragicomic side to one misfortune after another. This kind of humor is part of my life; it's how I see the world, through a mix of tears and laughter, but I'm unable to apply it to my periods of depression. There's no room for joking there, not even when experienced only as memory.

My depressive crisis neared an end only with yet another change in doctors. It was the third psychiatrist who finally found the right combination of medications, in addition to establishing a better dialogue with me. His name is Márcio dos Santos Melo. Like the previous doctors, Márcio changed up both my antidepressant and my mood stabilizer. I must have tried at least five antidepressants and three or four mood stabilizers in a single year. This time, it worked. The most interesting part about Márcio is that it was André who recommended him. He was also my father's psychiatrist. Considering that, as they say, mental illness can also be genetic, I decided to try my luck with the doctor who had been successfully treating my father. But soon after we began to hit our stride, Márcio informed me he was going to stop seeing patients. When he told me of his plans, I was doing better, but I was shocked. Márcio recommended a colleague, Euthymia Brandão de Almeida Prado, who has been a part of my life ever since. She made some final adjustments to the dosage of the medications that had set me on the right track and observed all of the resulting changes. Over time, she made additional adjustments as necessary, as is common in treating depression.

As the recent episode on the ski slopes shows, my depression hasn't abandoned me entirely. It remains dormant for months or years, but now and then appears in changes in sleep patterns, or as a result thereof. Beyond this, my medications still need to be adjusted now and then, on account of this or that chemical or psychological factor. The personal and professional protection of Euthymia, like that of Maria Elena before her, is of fundamental importance to this day. Without it, I wouldn't be writing these memoirs, or else the story would have a longer and more dramatic plotline.

I also began to exercise daily. Horseback riding, which I did for ten years, and running outside, which I still do, have had indisputable therapeutic effects. You can add exercise to therapy and medication on the list of essential activities. If I stay inside, without sun and without the fresh air in the lungs or the adrenaline provided by athletics, my depression takes over and recovery takes longer.

MANY ARE THE MOMENTS when a victim of depression thinks he has recovered, or close to it, when that isn't the case. On such occasions, more intense therapy or a change

in medication can help. Now that I'm better, I am absolutely terrified of altering my medication, but sometimes
it needs to be done. With the latest change, I began to
use lithium. I had reservations about this medication, fear
even, because lithium tends to be associated with serious
mental health disorders. I began to take it in low doses
and discovered the best mood stabilizer I've ever tried.

Long before this, at a moment when I thought I
was doing fine, already back at work full time, I received
a phone call from Montblanc's Brazil office. It seemed
strange to me, but I decided to pick up anyway. I learned
that the pen and watch manufacturer had decided to
create a prize, to be presented annually to an important
figure in the cultural industry. I was the first recipient.
The winner received a limited-edition Montblanc pen,
adorned with a gemstone that was to change each year.
The models were always named in honor of a writer. I
was presented with one that had an emerald in the clip,
and the name of the model was Agatha Christie.

I was to receive my prize in a morning ceremony at the
Museu da Casa Brasileira, where I had held the launch
party for Companhia das Letras. I was ecstatic. I become
very shy at award ceremonies, but this one arrived at the

best possible time to give me a lift once and for all. I expected the ceremony to be more important than it was, with guests and journalists representing major cultural organizations. Much to my surprise, the crowd basically consisted of representatives from Montblanc's sales outlets for pens, watches, and leather briefcases around the country.

As we made our way from my house to the museum—the same path I'd traced with Lili and Júlia thirteen years earlier—I could already sense I wasn't doing so well; I gave my hand to Lili and we walked silently to the ceremony. Emotions were already running high, and the event had yet to begin. Since my diagnosis, or perhaps even earlier, Lili had learned how to detect, by the expression in my eyes, the way I'm feeling. We'd finally attained the ideal I'd always longed for, to be understood without having to say a thing. Our affection for and knowledge of each other had made this possible; my eyes, too, began to clearly express my condition, above all at moments of despondency or depression. In addition to a lowering of my voice, my gaze began to speak for itself, the same way my father's once did. Lili always says that my eyes begin to shrink at such moments; they seem reluctant to open, as though seeking protection from the light or feeling ashamed at a given situation. That was my state as I arrived at the award ceremony.

When we made it to the museum, I noticed that the event would take place in the same room where I'd launched the publishing house. I didn't recognize anyone in the audience. The prize was announced and then I was handed a microphone. I began to speak, but my voice failed me. My plan had been to offer your standard thank-you speech, but just then I changed course. I only remember saying that the publishing house had been launched in the same room. After that, my voice failed me. There I was at the edge of tears with people I had never met, to the horror of everyone present.

The Montblanc official in charge, noticing that something was wrong—that my meager remarks would not serve the company's marketing aims and were lost on the audience—snatched the microphone from my hands without any qualms. I hurried from the museum, nearly forgetting to take my pen.

Years later, when I wrote the stories that would become *Discourse on Some Blades of Grass*, this episode at the museum came to mind. One of them, which I called

"Memoir," follows an executive who "wins" a prize like Man of the Year that, differently from mine, has been bought by his marketing team. At the prize ceremony, when they turn it over to him, his voice fails him, and instead of talking about his business achievements, he begins to describe his art collection, especially the first important work he acquired, a seascape where, in the foreground, patches of grass appear in the middle of the sand. The description of the painting is based on the first important painting I bought for my own collection. He goes on to ask—himself and the audience—how the grass ended up there, in such arid terrain unfit for vegetation. This was the image I came upon to conclude the book of stories, a metaphor that also applies to literature more generally: something resilient that feeds off chance, in addition to sprouting forth and developing in unexpected ways.

The successful businessman's memoirs were composed of his recollection of moments from his childhood, which feature in the book, sometimes spread across characters quite different from him: plumbers, washerwomen, doughnut vendors . . .

As the protagonist is waxing philosophical about the

grass in the sand, the microphone is snatched, just as it was from me. In the story, however, it is the marketing team from his conglomerate of businesses that takes this initiative, and they then begin to enumerate his accomplishments as an entrepreneur. Listening to what is said of him at the microphone, the businessman asks himself who might write a biography that would capture those events he would like to tell. It then occurs to him that he would prefer to write his memoirs rather than be the subject of a biography. The book would include the story of when he went to school alone for the first time and got off at the wrong bus stop, missing class because he arrived after the bell. He would also describe his first visit to a prostitute, in which he left the room in a fury after being called a little baby in bed. As the story comes to a close, he says that if the book ever comes to pass, its title would be *Discourse on Some Blades of Grass*.

And so the stories that readers of *Discourse on Some Blades of Grass* hold in their hands, and which carry on about (my) childhood, about my father and my family, or about the lives of characters who are hardly lofty figures, were in fact the memoirs of the businessman in question.

THERE WAS NO WAY I could leave out this last text of mine, given that it made it to publication—though today I'm unsure I would send it to press. As I venture to write these partial memoirs here, my protagonist, the depressed businessman, seems to make more sense.

In this book, I chose only to tell of my childhood and connect it to depression. I don't feel at ease to write about what I've achieved at Brasiliense or at Companhia das Letras. I've told of some of my experiences on the Companhia blog, but have always directed my letters to young editors, or to the reader interested in the book life in Brazil. I was true to my character in *Discourse on Some Blades of Grass*.

For this reason, as I conceived of these memoirs, I thought they ought to close with the launch of Companhia das Letras, despite the fact that the publishing house appears here and there, in the comings and goings of my narrative. I wanted to make it clear by the end that this is a book about a very particular childhood, about an illness that impacts my family life in various ways, and in a certain sense about an endless search, connected to my father, that I sought to transform into literary works on numerous occasions, a search that needed to take on a different form. I have made no secret of my social standing in this book. But depression affects people of all classes. The wealthiest are in a better position to identify and treat it. When it comes to health care, as with everything else, Brazil is a profoundly unjust country.

The story of my depression is what lurks behind a tale of success, which does not appear here. To make the scope of this book clear, I would like to close by telling exactly what happened at the launch of the publishing house, that is, on the eve of the birth of the thing that the majority of those who know me tie to my life story.

I HAD RECENTLY RETURNED from my first Frankfurt Book Fair for Companhia das Letras. We had yet to publish a single book, but already we had garnered some attention. I was more or less known in the press for my work at Brasiliense, and I was launching a new literary publisher, with its own unique visual identity, an expression of respect for the work of its authors. At the fair, I experienced a serious health issue. Riding in a taxi to the second day of the fair, I began to feel the intense pain characteristic of a kidney problem. The driver ignored my pleas for help. On the way to the Brazil stand, I collapsed under the weight of the pain. An editor I knew was walking just ahead of me, but I was unable to call out to her.

With some effort, I reached the stand and was sent directly to the hospital. I spent two days there. The doctors spoke only German and said with their hands that my left kidney had shifted to my pelvic region. Up to that point, I hadn't known that I had a congenital pelvic kidney. They would not release me even with the pain under control. My father had to come from Brazil to pick me up. I remember the look of pride on his face as he walked alongside me at the fair that Saturday before we both boarded the plane home.

When I made it back to Brazil, I sought out a doctor, but he couldn't explain whether I'd had a kidney stone or something else related to my pelvic kidney. Some days later, as a consequence of the kidney problem, a urinary tract infection snuck up on me.

The launch of the publishing house was to take place at the Museu da Casa Brasileira. That same night, there was a campaign dinner for future president of Brazil

Fernando Henrique Cardoso, who was then running for mayor of São Paulo, at the Clube Pinheiros, across the street from the museum.

The launch of Companhia das Letras had garnered much more attention than we had dreamed it would, and numerous individuals who had gone to the dinner for Cardoso decided to cross the street for our event. And so, half an hour after we arrived, the museum was buzzing with people. There were ten times as many guests as we were expecting.

I remember walking to the museum. Lili and Júlia were glowing, and I was very nervous. Pedro was only a year old and couldn't go. I can picture myself giving him a kiss as the three of us left to walk the two blocks down Avenida Brigadeiro Faria Lima to the museum as vividly as if it were a short time ago. Sometimes, I think back to Júlia on that day and picture my granddaughters in her place. Zizi and Alice are enthusiastic readers, and today they are such an important part of my life that I often picture one or the other donning the red-and-white floral dress and red shoes that their mother wore.

When we got to the event, my urinary tract infection got worse. Perhaps, adding to my nerves at that moment, it was trying to demand my undivided attention. I spent much of the time in the bathroom, where I would go every five minutes, while my family and the very first Companhia employees received guests in my place with gallantry.

When my body finally gave me a break, I would leave the bathroom and go back to the party. It was like I was arriving at the launch of Companhia das Letras every five minutes and, looking around at that crowd of people, asking myself: What is going on here?

THE ABSENT MOON

The clandestine organization where Tomás had enlisted hadn't always sympathized with the activities of the Swedish leader, who was viewed with a certain distrust. Wallenberg had initially obtained permission from the Hungarian government and from Eichmann to issue forty-five hundred passes so that Jews, either Swedish descendants or otherwise having close relations to his country, could leave Hungary. While arrangements were being made for this group's emigration, the Swedish embassy lodged those under its care no longer in residences bearing the Star of David but in rented houses, on whose facades the yellow-and-blue flag hung. Otto was charged with raising flagpoles and hoisting Swedish flags at several spots throughout Budapest. The Hungarian Nazi forces, known as the Arrow Cross Party, frequently violated the agreement with Wallenberg's government and attacked these supposed shelters. They also violated numerous armistices in their war against the Jews, designed to slow deportation. With time, Otto became one of Wallenberg's right-hand men. He saw to the issuance of passes, drove embassy vehicles, and carried supplies to the Jews under his leader's protection. Meanwhile, the group of partisans to which Tomás belonged falsified Wallenberg's passes, distributing them widely. These passes were poor counterfeits and interfered with the Swedish embassy's initial work, providing the Nazis with ammunition against the efforts of the playboy-cum-diplomat. It's possible that Otto had collaborated with his friend Tomás, smuggling passes to be reproduced with the rudimentary copy machines belonging to Budapest's fledgling Jewish resistance. Later on, Eichmann was successful in gaining the Hungarian government's permission for the mass deportation of more than five hundred thousand Jews. At this point, even Wallenberg had stopped caring about the falsified passes and had begun to follow the Jews on their death marches, handing out previously nonexistent safe-conducts himself, pretending to know each of the deportees, one by one, trying to free them from the trail that would lead to the gas chambers at Auschwitz, Birkenau, and Bergen-Belsen. Otto had his own moments of heroism, when he joined his boss in facing down the Arrow Cross battalions, who threatened the Jews with bayonets as they marched along. With all this political back-and-forth, each time Wallenberg won a round in his fight against Eichmann and the delivery of Jews to extermination camps eased, these Hungarian Nazi fanatics sprang into action and took it upon themselves to carry out more public executions. These were done by firing squad, the victims chosen at random, or by tossing ghetto dwellers into the gelid Danube, strapping a survivor to a recently executed Jew. One Jew, executed by gunshot, carried another Jew to a death by drowning. It's said that by morning, the waters of the Danube began to glow red during spates of Arrow Cross executions. The firing squads took place in the middle of the night, causing people to comment that the moonlight was never so absent from Budapest. When one more death by firing squad came to light, in one alley or another, Lajos looked to the heavens and prayed for the moon to shine brighter that night, to protect his family, his friends, and Jews everywhere—what use was a moon whose absence made it complicit in such massacres?

The passage above belongs to the novel The Absent Moon, never published, which mixes events from my father's life with a life I imagined for him, among other fictional moments. András appears in this story as Tomás, but Lajos, my grandfather, is Lajos. It is the grandfather I never met who prays for the moon to shine.

In this work of fiction, his prayer crosses three generations. I suppose in some sense I would like that a man as religious as my grandfather, wherever he is, keep my family in his prayers. I carry his name and his tallit, but I know him from only a single photo, in which he casts a serious look toward the camera. No doubt Lajos prayed for the son he pushed from the train. He would never have imagined he would have a Brazilian grandson, great-granddaughter, great-grandson, and great-great-granddaughters. He would no doubt be pleased to know that I go to the synagogue and that some of my family members also go. I am certain, however, that when it comes to religion, he would find my efforts lacking.

On a stroll soon after finishing the first draft of this book, it occurred to me that the feeling I have long had of reaching for air and not finding it available for me to breathe felt much like looking up in a night sky and finding no moon. That correspondence is also a tie between the lives of my grandfather and father and my own.

My intent with this book was not to address the hereditary component of depression, which has been carefully detailed in scientific books and medical pamphlets. Still, we know that there are triggers that activate—or do not—something that is in our DNA. If depression were simply hereditary, it would be much easier to treat. I also know that there are books that connect bipolar disorder to factors that led humanity's geniuses to sublime forms of intellectual and artistic expression. I have always reacted badly to this idea, and in the end I have not read most of the related literature. It might seem that I am committing an injustice in not doing so, but it is my belief that the creativity of great artists and thinkers does not derive exclusively or even predominantly from manic energy. Not even average obsessive career professionals like me ought to thank their bipolar traits for their productivity. For me, suffering is the only result of the illness at the center of this book. I am not part of any bipolar pride group, and I deeply regret the anguish that I caused, much of it stemming from this condition.

My father's own silence and depression generated a long search within myself. It is for this reason that he appears in so much of my writing. It is for this reason that I still seek him out at the synagogue, at dinners on Shabbat, at the cemetery, when I was visiting his two friends at their nursing home, and in so many other places. It is for this reason that I mourned him for so long.

My mother is alive, strong, and of sound mind. Our relationship now is beautiful and full. When my parents would fight, I didn't always accord her the admiration she deserved. Even without taking sides, perhaps I tended to give greater attention to the side I considered the underdog. Today, I hope I can make up for all of this. Assailed by problems with her mother and her husband, Mirta leaned on her father and on me. She resigned herself to the loss of her children and the woes of married life. But perhaps her happiness in old age can make up for all she went through.

Many times I hear people say that I am more and more like André. I can't say, but I know that I speak sparingly and in a low voice, just as he did. That my eyes transmit my sadness, as my father's did, even if they do so in their own way.

This book was built upon a long history of silences. The silence found in Lajos's personality, in his clandestine synagogue, in his life as a prisoner of a concentration camp. André's lasting silence after allowing his father to save him as he marched toward his death at Bergen-Belsen. My silence as an only child and only grandchild fearful of my parents' fragility. And now, though my depression is under control, there is much more silence in my life. This is not only a consequence of all I've experienced. It is also a choice. Silence is useful in my line of work. Reading takes place in silence and the work of an editor is basically to know how to read.

This being the case, my professional contributions certainly derive from the calculated application of silence. Writing this book is one more detour in my journey. It is a response to lacunae in my relationship with my father, and reflects no desire to see our roles reversed. After the books of stories and the frustrated attempt to write a novel based on my father's life, I promised myself that I would content myself with being merely a good reader. But the stories told here were in need of an outlet.

Here I no longer resort to fictions to fill my father's silence. I share my silence with those who wish to know the stories that belong to Lajos, András, and me.

In the hope that I might now go back to reading.

São Paulo, September 2020

Acknowledgments

In my coming to write this book, some very important people provided encouragement. The first, with whom I've lost contact, was the former Penguin Random House editor in Mexico, Ricardo Cayuela, who, during a meeting of the company's Latin American houses, hearing that I was trying to write a novel about my father, told me that what I really ought to do was write a work of nonfiction. His opinion whirled around my head for years.

Drauzio Varella, more recently, in a lunch at which I mentioned my desire to address my depression in a book, was resolute and emphatic. He urged me to write and reveal the unknown aspects of what, on the surface, was a successful life. When I began, after the events on the ski run, he was a close companion, always offering an encouraging word. When the first draft was finished, in the midst of the

COVID-19 pandemic, he asked to read it. Drauzio was the busiest man in the country but still found the time to give notes on a preliminary version of this book. Without his company, from the moment in which these memoirs were little more than a vague desire to the final text, this book would not have happened.

I owe everything that's ever gone right in life to Lili—as the reader of this book must have noticed. She knows me so well that whenever I do something, I can't tell whether I'm in control or if I'm merely a robot of her kindness and love. There is no way to explain what our renewed acquaintance— when I was not yet seventeen and she was only fifteen—has brought to my life. To this day, the anniversary of our first trip to the Cine Bijou to watch the film version of modernist literary masterpiece *Macunaíma* is way more important than my own birthday. It was there that the person I am today was born—better yet, the good side of who I am. Lili always wanted me to write more, and she showed herself to be a rigorous reader when the time came yet again.

Júlia and Pedro did the same. My children also read more than one draft and supported me throughout my hesitations and anxieties. All three contributed greatly to the final result. They also contributed even before the book was written, in a much more important way. I won my battle with depression thanks to Lili, Júlia, and Pedro—thanks to the tenderness they showed then and continue to show to this day in ever greater doses. I hope that reading this account has been motive for more happiness than sadness, though reliving such moments has not been easy for any of us. But transforming such sadness into a book is perhaps the happiest of endings to this story.

The initial group of readers for this book also included Maria Elena Salles and Euthymia Brandão de Almeida Prado. In the course of these memoirs, it comes clear that they were and remain guardian angels. Euthymia offered valuable suggestions from a medical point of view. The contributions of both have compelled me to offer yet more well-deserved thanks to the gratitude I already owed them. Many years after my depression, after my psychoanalysis had come to an end, an existential crisis brought me back to therapy. At the time, Luiz Meyer helped me and kept me from a more serious relapse.

Luiz Orenstein expressed interest in giving this a quick read and was, as always, a very involved friend. He read it with compassion, in a single night, and helped me to remain at peace with its publication. João Moreira Salles read with redoubled attention and gave me the gift of keen critiques and unrivaled generosity. Carlos Jardim, a friend I've gained only recently, gave me encouragement at a crucial point. Bernardo Carvalho and Michel Laub, upon learning that I was writing, offered their help and excellent suggestions. Sidarta Ribeiro provided his gift as a deeply empathetic reader.

Otávio Marques da Costa, Ricardo Teperman, Matinas Suzuki Jr., and Marcelo Ferroni are also among the very first readers of this book. I received from each of them great encouragement, tempered with the critiques that my work deserved.

Otávio and Ricardo followed through with suggestions until the end of the process, all of them excellent. They changed the course of the book significantly. They dealt with a very difficult author; after all, the shoemaker's son always goes barefoot . . . Any shortcomings of this book no doubt result from suggestions I did not follow. Lucila Lombardi and Daniela Duarte read the first chapters and were very receptive to this more-off-than-on writer. Mariana Figueiredo read with the generosity of a friend and great professional seriousness.

Any merits the original Portuguese edition of this work may have I owe to Márcia Copola, who was unflinching in her copyedits. Lucila, yet again, produced excellent work.

Alceu Nunes took care of this book and, with his mix of skill and friendship, gave it the look I longed for—visually discreet and pristine.

Scott Moyers was always a supporter of the idea of the book and worked to make it much better than the original text. I learned a lot about my job watching Scott and his team work. Many thanks indeed. Eric Becker's very good translation helped Scott's task. To my agents Bill Clegg and Marion Duvert I now owe a broader understanding of the word *generosity*. I thank them all, so very much.

Simon Krauz and Magda Vadás, two friends of my father's whom I spoke with to reconstruct his story, were always very generous and full of tenderness. They liked my father a great deal and transferred a portion of this love to me. When I finished the book, I called Magda at the senior home where she lived. I spoke with her by telephone, because visits were suspended. Her caretaker told me then that Simon had died of COVID-19 at the outset of the pandemic. I did not bring this detail to the book; I wanted to create a record of "Shimi" while he was still alive. My intention was to keep the description of my last visit, when, yet again, he initially took me for André, and told me that my father was the best man he had ever known. Now even Magda is not with us anymore. The passing of those close friends who fought in the war and migrated to Brazil together with András mean a lot to this history.

My cousin, Tom Lanny, helped me with many precious details. Sometimes we have different outlooks on life, but these differences are much smaller than the great love that unites us. We are each other's only cousin. Writing this book brought us even closer.

To those who are no longer with us—Giuseppe, Mici, and André—I dedicate further declarations of love. I am an endless depository of affection and gratitude for all that you gave me.

I wanted to save a few words for my two granddaughters, Zizi and Alice, who are responsible for a great deal of my current happiness. If one day you read this book, I hope you understand Grandpa as a guy with strong emotions, who faced some difficult moments but now has won the prize of having both of you so present in his life to share incredible travels, daily GIFs, movies, music, and long talks. My most important role in life today is to witness the smiles and intelligence so particular to each of you. I thank Luiz Henrique Schwarcz Ligabue for the long chats and fine food.

ACKNOWLEDGMENTS

A FEW SHORT MONTHS after I wrote the first version of this book, Mirta was hospitalized with COVID-19. During the twenty or so days she was in the hospital, only one person was allowed to accompany her. I spent nearly twelve hours a day at my mother's side until she was released. After the initial frightening days, when she had begun to feel better, we spoke at length and she shared story after story. At a certain point, she said that what we were experiencing was like a repeat of a time more than fifty years ago. As she remembered it, at that time I was there at her bedside giving her milk with a medicine dropper, or in tiny spoons, on account of the ulcer that had beset her along with the series of miscarriages. The hours I spent at her side as a child during her numerous recovery stints are a central part of this book. For this reason, I dedicate the most special of acknowledgments to her.

Mirta read the first draft of this book twice. After the shock of the first reading, she embarked on another, more serene reading, after which she gave me her total blessing to the publication of this story. Hers was a courageous, generous stance, full of wisdom. As always, my mother wanted the best for me. I have no way to thank her at this point, for everything, since the day I was born.

P.S. Finally, I send my greatest love to Bartolomeu, wherever he may be. I will never forget the hours at your side, nor the unmatched tenderness of your canine kisses! And for Margot, for whom I am now able to cry.

P.P.S. I had two special companions during the writing of this book: Ludwig van Beethoven and Giacomo Puccini. I decided I would work only to the sounds of these two composers. This rendered the writing at once more profound and more gratifying.